TION

OF CALVIN'S
BIRTHDAY

JOHN CALVIN:
HIS LIFE AND INFLUENCE

John Calvin has had his detractors ever since his own day in the mid-sixteenth century right down to the approach to the 500th anniversary of his birth in the early twenty-first century. But these are mostly opponents of the gospel of Jesus Christ or people who have not taken the time to understand his writings or to get to know the man. Dr. Reymond tells the story of Calvin's life and thought in a compact and compelling way that will serve to acquaint readers with the warm human character of Calvin and make them want to study his writings. His description of Calvin's masterful statement at the Lausanne Disputation of 1536 is by itself worth the price of the book.

Dr. William S. Barker
Professor of Church History, Emeritus
Westminster Theological Seminary, Philadelphia, Pennsylvania

Theologian Robert Reymond (author of *A New Systematic Theology of the Christian Faith*) sets forth the life of John Calvin in four chapters (originally four lectures given at the Coral Ridge Presbyterian Church in Fort Lauderdale, Florida). Reymond's book is succinct and comprehensive, appreciative and probing, historical and theological, scholarly and pastoral. Especially valuable is Reymond's treatment of the burning of Servetus in which he summarizes William Cunningham's five considerations that ameliorate to some degree Calvin's involvement in the tragedy – and adds eight further points of his own. There are three appendices including a useful annotated list of recommended Calvin biographies.

Dr. David B. Calhoun,
Professor of Church History,
Covenant Theological Seminary, St Louis, Missouri

This refreshing new book about John Calvin, from a highly respected author and educator at Knox Theological Seminary, deserves the serious attention of all who call themselves Presbyterians. Dr. Reymond sheds new light on a famous and familiar name. His writing style is scholarly and authoritative, but at the same time anecdotal and intensely interesting reading. It belongs in every church library where access is afforded to theologian and layman alike.

The late Dr. D. James Kennedy,
Senior Minister,
Coral Ridge Presbyterian Church, Fort Lauderdale, Florida

JOHN CALVIN:
HIS LIFE AND INFLUENCE

Robert L. Reymond

Robert L. Reymond is Emeritus Professor of Systematic Theology at Knox Theological Seminary, Fort Lauderdale Florida. Prior to Knox, Dr. Reymond taught 22 years at Covenant Theological Seminary in St. Louis. He has lectured in Korea, Japan, England, Scotland, Israel, Jamaica, Malawi, and South Africa, and has served pastorates in Tennessee, Georgia, Missouri, and Illinois. He has authored numerous books including:

John - Beloved Disciple (ISBN 1-85792-628-5),
Paul - Missionary Theologian (ISBN 9781-85792-497-5)
Jesus - Divine Messiah (ISBN 978-1-85792-802-0)
What is God? (ISBN 978-1-4550-228-7)
Contending for the Faith (ISBN 978-1-84550-045-0)
The Lamb of God (ISBN 978-1-84550-181-0)
The God-centered Preacher (ISBN 978-1-85792-896-9)
Faith's Reasons for Believing (ISBN 978-1-84550-337-6)

©Robert L. Reymond 2004
ISBN 978-1-85792-966-9

Published in 2004
reprinted 2008
by
Christian Focus Publications,
Geanies House, Fearn, Ross-shire
IV20 1TW, Great Britain.

www.christianfocus.com

Edited by Malcolm Maclean
Cover design by Alister MacInnes
Printed by CPD Wales

CONTENTS

DEDICATION

To
William Mackenzie,
Publisher of Christian Focus Publications, who
—like Thomas Platter and Balthasar Lasius of Basle in 1536,
Wendelin Rihel of Strasbourg in 1539, 1543, and 1545,
Jean Gerard of Geneva in 1550, and
Robert Stevens (Estienne) of Geneva in 1553 and 1559,
who published the several Latin editions of John Calvin's
Institutes of the Christian Religion—
has published in our times the works of numerous authors
who stand in the tradition of the great Genevan Reformer,
I dedicate with appreciation
this book.

PREFACE

This monograph contains with some minor revisions and additions the four popular lectures that I gave to a large audience at the Coral Ridge Presbyterian Church in Fort Lauderdale, Florida on consecutive Wednesday evenings in February 2002.

Just as Abraham Kuyper, when invited to give the Stone Lectures at Princeton University in 1898, "could not hesitate a moment as to my choice of subject," namely, the subject of Calvinism,[1] so also I, having been granted my choice of topics for the series by the minister in charge of the four evening meetings, in less than twenty-four hours of reflection chose for my lecture topic the life and influence of John Calvin, the sixteenth-century Protestant Reformer, both because of his immeasurable (and continuing) historical and theological influence on the world and because the average twenty-first-century Christian knows very little about him and all too often what they do know or have heard about him has been badly distorted. The words "Calvin" and "Calvinism" evoke ideas of the "reign" of a religious dictator in sixteenth-century Geneva or perhaps of God "manipulating" his creatures either to heaven or to hell.

So from lecture material for my course, "Calvin's *Institutes*," that I offer at Knox Theological Seminary, I wrote the four lectures, taking my original audience on a journey through Calvin's intellectual and spiritual

---

[1]Abraham Kuyper, *Lectures on Calvinism* (Grand Rapids: Eerdmans, 1931), 12.

development, first from his youth, then through young manhood, then to the brilliant, energetic young Reformer that he became during his first Geneva period, and finally to the maturer Reformer into which he developed, first at Strasbourg, and then during his second Geneva period. In connection with this last period I addressed head-on Calvin's part in the most significant blight on Protestant Geneva's reputation, namely, the burning of Michael Servetus.

It will be obvious to my readers who are familiar with the Calvin literature that I have "fished in many waters" for the factual information contained herein. I make no pretense that this work plows totally new ground unless it be in the selection and arrangement of the material. Rather, it attempts, as the title implies, to introduce the reader who is unfamiliar with Calvin to this amazing Frenchman and his thought and major accomplishments. I only request that the Calvin scholar who might honor me by reading this monograph would remember that no author can say everything he would like to say about Calvin in four hour-long lectures.

I have tried to give credit in the footnotes to those Calvin biographers who have made some unique observation about him or who have reported some interesting detail about Calvin beyond those that all his biographers record. To keep the lectures "user-friendly" for the theological beginner I have placed where I could the more technical information in the footnotes. Of course, I did not read the informational footnotes when I delivered these lectures to their original audience, but readers should definitely read them. In my opinion, they contain much valuable information, especially about other prominent reformers of the time.

I offer these expanded lectures now to the broader Christian reading public in the hope that, as the Reformed world approaches the fifth centennial celebration of Calvin's birth on July 10, 2009, this remarkable Frenchman's life and ministry will challenge Protestant Christians today to take more interest in their historical heritage and to read for themselves "the *opus magnum* of Christian theology"[2] and the most influential systematic theology ever written, namely, John Calvin's *Institutes of the Christian Religion*.[3]

---

[2]John Murray, "Introduction," to Calvin's *Institutes of the Christian Religion*, translated by Henry Beveridge (Grand Rapids: Eerdmans, 1947), 1.

[3]Because of its freshness and footnotes I recommend Ford Lewis Battles' translation of Calvin's *Institutes of the Christian Religion*, edited by John T. McNeill and published simultaneously in 1960 as volumes XX and XXI in The Library of Christian Classics by the Westminster Press in the U. S. A. and the S. C. M. Press in Great Britain. Henry Beveridge's 1845 translation for the Calvin Translation Society, republished by Wm. B. Eerdmans Publishing Company in 1947, is also a fine, trustworthy translation.

CHAPTER ONE

GOD'S PREPARATION
OF THE FUTURE REFORMER

INTRODUCTION: CALVIN'S INSTITUTES

Jean Cauvin, Littérateur—"John Calvin, Author." This one-word description is the way a biographical sketch of his life could justly begin its depiction of John Calvin, for he was that all right—in spades![1] His fame as such began when he was twenty-six years old when from safe asylum in Basel, Switzerland he published in March of 1536 the first edition of his *Institutes of the Christian Religion*[2] comprising six lengthy chapters that went through ever-enlarging editions over his lifetime until it reached its final and definitive form of eighty chapters in 1559 when he was fifty years old.[3] Though he was constantly enlarging, reconsidering, and

---

[1]Calvin's writings appear in the *Corpus Reformatorum: Johannis Calvini Opera quae supersunt omnia*, edited by N. W. Baum, E. Cunitz, E. Reuss, P. Lobstein and A. Erichson (Brunswick and Berlin: C. A. Schweiske, 1863-1900) as volumes 29 through 87—fifty-nine large volumes in all! But even these do not exhaust Calvin's total literary output: twelve more volumes under the title *Supplementa Calviniana*, edited by E. Mulhaupt and others (Neukirchen: Neukirchener Verlag), are available.

[2]"Institutes" from the Latin *institutio* means "instruction," "manual," "summary." Thus Calvin's *Institutes* paralleled Quintilian's *Institutes of Oratory* and Erasmus' *Institutes of a Christian Prince*. "Pedagogy was the key to the entire Calvinist enterprise," Bernard Cottret rightly observes in his *Calvin: a Biography*, translated by M. Wallace McDonald (Grand Rapids: Eerdmans, 2000), 174.

[3]Subsequent Latin editions of the *Institutes* appeared in 1539, 1543, 1545, 1550, 1553, and 1554 until it reached its final form in 1559.

recasting his thought in the *Institutes*, the sentences that underwent major revision are not many while the substance remained consistently the same throughout. It has often been observed that the 1559 edition was simply the older man putting his seal on what the younger man had written twenty-three years earlier. In other words, Calvin did not have to write at the end of his life, as did Augustine, a *Retractations* in connection with his earlier editions of the *Institutes*.

What is one holding when he holds in his hands Calvin's *Institutes*—the work more fiercely and persistently opposed than any other work of the sixteenth century and twice ordered by the Sorbonne to be burned, which burnings occurred in 1542 and 1544 in front of Notre Dame Cathedral in Paris, the work that one Roman Catholic authority of the day vilified as "the Koran or rather the Talmud of heresy,"[4] the work whose author became Rome's most hated enemy, the work described by Will Durant, a twentieth-century American historian, as "the most eloquent, fervent, lucid, logical, influential, and terrible…in all the literature of the religious revolution…developing the thought of [its author's] predecessors to ruinously logical conclusions," whose author, because of his doctrine of predestination, "darkened the human soul with the most absurd and blasphemous conception of God in all the long and honored history of nonsense"?[5]

Other authorities, I am pleased to note, urge another opinion. Benjamin B. Warfield, the early-twentieth-century professor of didactic and polemic theology at Princeton

---

[4]Florimond de Raemond, counsellor of the Parlement of Bordeaux, *Historie de la naissance, progrez ed decadence l'hérésie de ce siècle* (Paris, 1605).

[5]Will Durant, *The Reformation*, in *The Story of Civilization* (New York: MJF, n.d.), Volume 6: 460, 465, 490. See Appendix A for more negative comments about Calvin and his ministry.

Theological Seminary, answered my question about Calvin's *Institutes* this way:

> As the first adequate statement of the positive programme of the Reformation movement, the 'Institutes' lies at the foundation of the whole development of Protestant theology, and has left an impress on evangelical thought which is ineffaceable. After three centuries and a half [Warfield was writing in 1909, the four hundredth anniversary year of Calvin's birth], it retains its unquestioned preeminence as the greatest and most influential of all dogmatic treatises. "There," said Albrecht Ritschl, pointing to it, "There is the masterpiece of Protestant theology."[6]

In a second article Warfield declares:

> [The *Institutes*] was the first serious attempt to cast into systematic form that body of truth to which the Reformed churches adhered as taught in the Holy Scriptures; and as such it met a crisis and created an epoch in the history of the Churches. In the immense upheaval of the Reformation movement, the foundations of the faith seemed to many to be broken up, and the most important questions to be set adrift; extravagances of all sorts sprang up on every side; and we can scarcely wonder that a feeling of uneasiness was abroad, and men were asking with concern for some firm standing-ground for their feet. It was Calvin's 'Institutes' which, with its calm, clear, positive expositions of the evangelical faith on the irrefragable authority of the Holy Scriptures, gave stability to wavering minds, and confidence to sinking hearts, and placed upon the lips of all a brilliant apology, in the face of the calumnies of the enemies of the Reformation.
>
> As the fundamental treatise in the development of a truly evangelical theology its mission has stretched, however, far beyond its own day. All subsequent attempts to state and defend that

---

[6]Benjamin B. Warfield, "John Calvin: The Man and His Work," *The Works of Benjamin B. Warfield* (Reprint; Grand Rapids: Baker, 1991), V, 8-9.

theology necessarily go back to it as their starting-point, and its impress upon the history of evangelical thinking is ineffaceable. Even from the point of view of mere literature, it holds a position so supreme in its class that every one who would fain know the world's best books, must make himself familiar with it. What Thucydides is among Greek, or [Edward] Gibbon among eighteenth century English historians, what Plato is among philosophers, or the Iliad among epics, or Shakespeare among dramatists, that Calvin's 'Institutes' is among theological treatises.[7]

In yet a third article Warfield states:

The publication of [the *Institutes of the Christian Religion*] was like the setting up of the King's Standard in Mediaeval Europe— that the lieges might gather to it. It was raising the banner on high that all men might see it and rally around it. It provided at last a platform for the hard-bestead [badly situated] Protestants, everywhere spoken against, and far too easily confounded with the radicals of the day—radicals who scouted the very foundations of the Christian faith, overturned the whole fabric of the social order, outraged the commonest dictates of ordinary decency. Its publication met a crisis and created an epoch. It gave a new stability to Protestantism, and set it before the world as a coherent system of reasoned truth by which men might live and for which they might gladly die.[8]

William Cunningham, the renowned nineteenth-century Scottish Reformed theologian (to whom, states Warfield, we should happily concede the right to have an opinion on the matter), declares:

---

[7]Warfield, "On the Literary History of Calvin's 'Institutes,'" *Works*, V, 373-4.

[8]Warfield, "Calvin and the Reformation," in *Selected Shorter Writings of Benjamin B. Warfield,* edited by John E. Meeter (Nutley, N.J., Presbyterian and Reformed, 1970), I, 403-4.

The 'Institutio' of Calvin is the most important work in the history of theological science, that which is more than any other creditable to its author, and has exerted directly or indirectly the greatest and most beneficial influence upon the opinions of intelligent men on theological subjects. It may be said to occupy, in the science of theology, the place which it requires both the 'Novum Organum' of [Francis] Bacon, and the 'Principia of Newton' to fill up, in physical science,—at once conveying, though not in formal didactic precepts and rules, the finest idea of the way and manner in which the truths of God's word ought to be classified and systematized, and at the same time actually classifying and systematizing them, in a way that has not yet received any very material or essential improvement. There had been previous attempts to present the truths of Scripture in a systematic form and arrangement, and to exhibit their relations and mutual dependence. But all former attempts had been characterized by great defects and imperfections; and especially all of them had been more or less defective in this most important respect, that a considerable portion of the materials, of which they were composed, had been not truths but errors,—not the doctrines actually taught in the sacred Scriptures, but errors arising from ignorance of the contents of the inspired volume, or from serious mistakes, as to the meaning of its statements. One of the earlier attempts at a formal system of theology was made in the eighth century, by Johannes Damascenus, and this is a very defective and erroneous work. The others which had preceded Calvin's 'Institutes,' in this department, were chiefly the productions of the schoolmen, Lombard's four books of 'Sentences,' and Thomas Aquinas's 'Summa,' with the commentaries upon these works; and they all exhibited very defective and erroneous views of scriptural truth.... The first edition of Melanchthon's 'Common Places,'—the only one published before Calvin produced the first edition of his 'Institutes'—was not to be compared to Calvin's work, in the accuracy of its representation of the doctrines of Scripture, in the fulness and completeness of its materials, or in the skill and ability with which they were digested and arranged; and in the subsequent editions [of the 'Common Places'], while the inaccuracy increased in some respects rather than diminished, it still continued, to a considerable extent, a defective and ill digested work, characterized by a good deal of prolixity and wearisome repetition. It was in these circumstances that Calvin produced his 'Institutes,' the materials of which it was composed being in almost every instance the true doctrines really taught in the word of God, and exhibiting the whole substance of what is taught there on matters of doctrine, worship, government, and discipline,—and the whole of these materials being arranged with admirable skill and expounded in their meaning, evidence, and bearings, with consummate ability. This was the great and peculiar service which Calvin rendered to the cause of truth and the interests of sound theology, and its value and importance it is scarcely possible to overrate...In this work...Calvin was far above the weakness of aiming at the invention of novelties in theology, or of wishing to be regarded as the discoverer of new opinions. The main feature of the representation which he put forth of the scheme of divine truth, might be found in the writings of Augustine and Luther,—in neither singly, but in the two conjointly. But by grasping with vigour and comprehensiveness the whole scheme of divine truth and all its various departments, and combining them into one harmonious and well-digested system, he has done what neither Augustine nor Luther did or could have done, and has given conclusive evidence that he was possessed of the highest intellectual powers, as well as enjoyed the most abundant communications of God's Spirit.[9]

The original Strasbourg editors of Calvin's complete works stated in the mid-nineteenth century:

...though Luther was supremely great as a man and Zwingli was second to none as a Christian citizen, and Melanchthon well deserves the appellation of the most learned of teachers, Calvin may justly be called the leader and standard-bearer of theologians. For who will not marvel at his command of language and letters, at

---

[9]William Cunningham, "John Calvin," *The Reformers and the Theology of the Reformation* (Edinburgh: Banner of Truth, 1967), 295-97.

his control of the entire sphere of learning? The abundance of his learning, the admirable disposition of his material, the force and validity of his reasoning in dogmatics, the acuteness and subtlety of his mind, and the alternating gay and biting saltness of his polemics, the felicitous perspicuity, sobriety and sagacity of his exegetics, the nervous eloquence and freedom of his paraenetics, his incomparable legislative prudence and wisdom in the constitution, ordering and governing of the churches—all this is fully recognized among men of learning and candor. Even among the Romish controversialists themselves, there is none to-day possessed of even a moderate knowledge of these matters or endowed with the least fairness in judgment, who does not admire the richness of his reasoning and ideas, the precision of his language, the weight and clearness of his diction, whether in Latin or French. All these qualities are, of course, present in his other writings, but they are especially striking in that immortal *Institutes of the Christian Religion*, which beyond all controversy far excels all expositions of the kind that have been written from the days of the apostles down, including, of course, Melanchthon's *Loci Theologici*; and which captivates even to-day the learned and candid reader, even though he may be committed to different opinions, and wrests from him an unwilling admiration...none of [Calvin's other] writings is superior to [the *Institutes*] in the fame it enjoys. It has often happened that a book distinguished by the great applause of men has afterwards fallen into neglect through the harsher judgment or the careless indifference of a later time; often, too, that one which reached few minds at first, and almost escaped notice, has, as time proceeded, emerged from obscurity and is daily celebrated with increasing praise. But with regard to [the *Institutes*], seized upon from its very cradle with great and widespread avidity, and scrutinized by its very adversaries with a zeal born of envy, its glory has abided the same, intact now through three centuries, without the least diminution or fading, despite the frequent changes which successive schools of theology have introduced into the treatment of Christian doctrine.[10]

---

[10]*Corpus Reformatorum: Johannis Calvini Opera quae supersunt omnia*, xxix, xxi.

John T. McNeill, professor emeritus of church history at
Union Theological Seminary (NY) and editor of the Ford
Lewis Battles' translation of the *Institutes* in the Library of
Christian Classics, declares that Calvin's *Institutes*

> holds a place in the short list of books that have notably affected
> the course of history, molding the beliefs and behavior of
> generations of mankind. Perhaps no other theological work
> has so consistently retained for four centuries a place on the
> reading list of studious Christians.... It has, from time to time,
> called forth an extensive literature of controversy. It has been
> assailed as presenting a harsh, austere, intolerant Christianity
> and so perverting the gospel of Christ, and it has been admired
> and defended as an incomparable exposition of Scriptural truth
> and a bulwark of evangelical faith. Even in times when it was
> least esteemed, its influence remained potent in the life of
> active churches and in the habits of men. To many Christians
> whose worship was proscribed under hostile governments, this
> book has supplied the courage to endure. Wherever in the
> crises of history social foundations are shaken and men's hearts
> quail, the pages of this classic are searched with fresh respect.
> In our generation, when most theological writers are schooled
> in the use of methods, and of a terminology, widely differing
> from those employed by Calvin, this masterpiece continues to
> challenge intensive study, and contributes a reviving impulse
> to thinking in the areas of Christian doctrine and social duty.[11]

To say the least, none of these later assessments of Calvin's
Institutes is, in my opinion, an overdrawn description of the
work. Calvin's *Institutes* was a work that was born in battle,
a missile that continued to be launched at Christ's enemies
through its several editions.

But before one can delve meaningfully into such a
magnificent literary work it is imperative that one know

---

[11]John T. McNeill, ed., *Calvin: Institutes of the Christian Religion*,
translated by Ford Lewis Battles (The Library of Christian Classics;
Philadelphia: Westminster, 1960), 1, xxix.

something about the author himself. This brief lecture series on Calvin's life will, I hope, provide enough information about him to make his *Institutes*, as you read and study it, more meaningful.

In this first lecture we want to trace as best we can, given the at times sparse data with which we have to work, the evident hand of divine providence in the preparation of the author of the *Institutes* for the great task to which God would some day call him.

THE YOUNG CALVIN AND HIS EARLY EDUCATION

John Calvin was born almost five hundred years ago on July 10, 1509 as the middle of three surviving sons of five (Charles, John, and Antoine), in Noyon in the northern French province of Picardy. His father, Gérard Cauvin, was a highly esteemed notary, solicitor to the bishop, and fiscal administrator and general *factotum* to the Noyon clergy, and his beautiful mother, Jeanne (Lefranc), was noted for her religious piety and motherly affection. She died when Calvin was still a little boy, but many years later, in his 1543 treatise on Catholic relics, he recalled that she took him to visit the abbey at Ourscamp, four miles south of Noyon, where he said he remembered kissing the alleged skull of St. Anne. In the Collège des Capettes, a school for Noyon children, Calvin early distinguished himself as having an extraordinary intellect and strength of character. Because of his father's personal achievements and social and church connections with the distinguished de Hangest and Montmor families of Noyon, Calvin was able to acquire in his youth a refinement of manners, a knowledge of polite society, and an aristocratic bearing which neither Martin Luther, the German Reformer, nor Ulrich Zwingli, the German-speaking Swiss Reformer, ever possessed and which prepared him to feel at home in the society of the earth's great ones, even with princes and kings.

To put his life's beginning in some kind of context I would note that Luther, born November 10, 1483,[12] and Zwingli, born almost two months later on January 1, 1484, were both already twenty-five years old when Calvin was born, and Philip Melanchthon, Luther's systematizer, was born February 16, 1497 and thus was Calvin's senior by twelve years. So clearly Calvin was a "second generation" Reformer who greatly benefited from the first Reformers' labors. His birth year was also the same year that Henry VIII of England, born in 1491, began his reign. When Calvin was not quite eight and a half years old Martin Luther nailed his Ninety-Five Theses to the door of the Castle Church in Wittenberg on October 31, 1517. Soon Lutheran ideas were penetrating into France. And the year before (1516), in German-speaking Switzerland, Zwingli was already preaching the gospel and bringing Reformation thought to Zürich independently of Luther.

Schooling At Paris

Because his father had destined Calvin at this time for the priesthood, it was arranged on May 19, 1521, when he was almost twelve years old, that he would receive a church benefice for educational purposes in Paris, consisting of a part of the revenue[13] of a chaplaincy in the cathedral of Noyon. At that same time he also received the tonsure (the shaving of the crown of the head), the church's rite of admission to the clerical state.

---

[12] The life and ministry of Martin Luther do not fall within the purview of this monograph. For the reader who would like to read about him and the reformation he spawned in the sixteenth century I would recommend Roland H. Bainton, *Here I Stand. A Life of Martin Luther* (Nashville: Abingdon-Cokesbury, 1950).

[13] This revenue consisted annually of three measures of corn from one town and the wheat of twenty grain fields from another.

Perhaps because of the plague in and around Noyon but surely primarily to provide for his son the best available education, Calvin's father arranged for John, also when he was almost twelve years of age,[14] to accompany the sons of the Montmors and the de Hangests, the two prominent Noyon families mentioned earlier, sixty miles south-southwest to Paris, to begin his studies in August 1521 at the University there, the most famous educational institution in Europe.[15] In Paris he probably lived with his uncle Richard, a locksmith. There is some question whether he enrolled at the Collège de la Marche or the Collège de Sainte-Barbe (two of the over fifty colleges that existed under the umbrella of the University of Paris) or even whether he enrolled at either, but in any event it is fairly certain that in Paris he entered the "grammar course" in preparation for the arts course in *philosophia* and then after that the course in theology.

The "grammar course" was three-staged: the first, which Calvin probably already had behind him when he matriculated, was Latin fundamentals; the second was Latin syntax with all the anomalies and irregularities of Latin; and the third was elementary logic in which he probably learned by heart the *summulae*, an abridgment of Aristotle's *Organon*, read some Latin poetry, and studied some arithmetic.[16] Divine providence arranged that for a time he would study Latin

---

[14]Here I am following T. H. L. Parker's "minority view" chronology that he advances in his *John Calvin: A Biography* (Philadelphia: Westminster, 1975), 4, 156-61. Parker puts Calvin's departure from Noyon for study in Paris as early as 1521 or even 1520 when he would have been eleven or even ten years old. The majority view has him leaving for Paris in 1523.

[15]Parker's portrayal of university life and studies in Paris in the early sixteen century (see his *John Calvin*, 4-16) is fuller than just about any other English biography of Calvin.

[16]Parker, *John Calvin*, 4-6.

and good French grammar under Mathurin Cordier, the best Latinist in France, who was teaching at La Marche at the time, whose concern was to purify the Latin of its French flavoring. Cordier was so attracted to his young pupil that many years later he came as an old man to Geneva to teach in the Academy Calvin founded there and Calvin dedicated his commentary on First Thessalonians to him.

Another teacher, Jacques Lefèvre d'Étaple, a reformer in the Roman church who never broke from the church, who had published in 1512 a commentary on Paul's letters in which he stressed a mystical devotion to Christ approaching the Reformation's Christocentrism[17] and in 1523 his own translation of the New Testament, was teaching at the Sorbonne at this time. While he did not teach Calvin he did teach, among other reform-minded men who might be mentioned, William Farel who later would become Calvin's senior co-worker during Calvin's first period of service in Geneva.

After about a year Calvin's father transferred him to the lice-ridden, filthy ecclesiastical Collège de Montaigu, another college of the University of Paris.[18] The college was under the governance of the strict, irascible Noël Bédier who forbade his students to speak in French and required

---

[17]Lefèvre never attained Luther's clarity on the doctrine of justification by faith alone and continued to believe in Mary's immaculate conception and in purgatory. As one historian has written, Lefèvre was "closer to the Reformers in his silences than in his words." See Philip Edgcumbe Hughes, *Lefèvre* (Grand Rapids: Eerdmans, 1984).

[18]Desiderius Erasmus had attended the Collège de Montaigu before Calvin in 1494 and Ignatius Loyola followed him there from 1528 to 1535. The visitor to Paris today should not try to find this college for it was destroyed shortly after the French Revolution. The Bibliothèque Sainte-Geneviève stands today on the site, but on the library's facade that faces the Pantheon one can find Calvin's name inscribed along with such names as Erasmus and Rabelais.

them to speak only in Latin. At Montaigu Calvin entered the arts program. Here he very probably studied under the Scottish disciple of Duns Scotus, conciliar theologian and historian, John Major (or Mair), one of the last and greatest of the late medieval scholastic scholars who—in spite of Calvin's later rejection of the papacy and its "schoolmen"— profoundly influenced Calvin's thought and actions to the last. Douglas F. Kelly states that Major

> combined an avid interest in civil questions and constitutional history with an erudite commitment to ancient Catholic theology.... [As a conciliarist theologian] he believed in the supreme authority of a general council of the church over the pope, with the foundational assumption that constitutional law is for the benefit of the people, rather than for the pleasure of the ruler.[19]

This conciliar, constitutional thought was later to become very important to Calvin and even more so to his French and Scottish followers. And while Calvin's later exegetical work was to become far more indebted to the humanist Renaissance thinkers, such as Budé and Erasmus, Major's hostility to medieval allegorical interpretations of Scripture in favor of its literal interpretation undoubtedly deeply influenced the young Calvin in his reading of Scripture and the other ancient texts. In yet one other way Major influenced Calvin's later theology: theology was to be a "practical" rather than a "speculative" science, and this practical nature of theology was to involve Calvin in activities and controversies that Major would never have dreamed of.

While at Montaigu Calvin also studied the medieval debate methods of *disputatio* and *quaestio* in preparation

---

[19]Douglas F. Kelly, *The Emergence of Liberty in the Modern World: The Influence of Calvin on Five Governments from the 16th through 18th Centuries* (Phillipsburg, New Jersey: Presbyterian and Reformed, 1992), 6.

for his "determinations," the oral exams of the Bachelor of
Arts degree, and very likely was required to read in Latin (and
virtually memorize) large portions of such classics as
Aristotle's *Organon* (on logic), *Physica* (on the natural
sciences), *de Anima* (on psychology), and *Metaphysica* (on
natural theology), Boethius' *Arithmetica*, Pierre d'Ailly's *de
Sphaera* (on natural science), John Pecham's *Perspectiva
Communis* (on optics), the first six books of Euclid, Ptolemy's
Almagest, Lombard's *Sentences*, and commentaries on these
works.

The logic in which he was schooled, which formed the
backbone of the arts program at Montaigu, was almost
certainly nominalist and terminist (having to do with the
linguistic analysis of terms).[20] Calvin would later describe
his training for the priesthood at this time in his "Reply to
Sadoleto" as

---

[20]According to Parker, *John Calvin*, 11-12, terminist logic—the
via moderna over against the *via antiqua* that one reads about in
the literature describing this period—and the terminist movement in
general were concerned with the analysis of the relationship between
language about objects, the mental conception of the object, and the
object itself. It involved a linguistic exercise, at first very simple but
then becoming highly complex, consisting chiefly in distinctions between
several sorts of terms. Correspondingly, it had its own quite barbarous
technical language—categorematic, syncatagorematic, absolute
categorematic, connotative categorematic, *terminus prolatus*,
terminus scriptus, *terminus conceptus*, first and second intentions,
and so on.
The ultimate concern of terminist logic was to understand the
relationship between a given term that either signifies or stands in
place of the object, the mental concept of the object mediated by the
term, and the object itself. The question was asked whether the term
genuinely signifies what it is intended to signify, even whether the
term can stand for its object. Another question had to do with the
validity of correspondence between the mental concept of the term
and the term itself, or what guarantee is there that the mental concept
genuinely corresponds to the object itself. The net effect of this

mere sophistry, and sophistry so twisted, involved, tortuous and puzzling that scholastic theology might well be described as a kind of esoteric magic. The denser the darkness in which anyone shrouded a subject and the more he puzzled himself and others with preposterous riddles, the greater his fame for acumen and learning.

Doubtless he also encountered Lutheran ideas, likely much distorted and maligned, while a student at Montaigu—after all, the Paris faculty had issued its *Determinatio* in 1521 in which it condemned one hundred and four propositions attributed to Luther—but whether these Lutheran ideas influenced him in any significant way is very doubtful. He seems still to have been a devout Roman Catholic at this time, receiving a second church benefice in 1527.

After three or so years Calvin received his Licentiate of Arts degree (equivalent to our M.A. degree) probably in 1525 or 1526 when he was sixteen or seventeen years old, for which honor an exception would have had to be made to the regulation that Licentiates had to be at least twenty-one years old.

---

terminist logic was first to make knowledge subjective, but subjectivist philosophy goes hand in hand with skepticism: Do I really know, can I really know the object itself? Do I stand in a true relationship with the object? If I know only the term, how can I know that the term genuinely represents the object? When this kind of logic is applied to religion, then theology in a real sense becomes impossible; all that can be done is simply to make dogmatic assertions. Little wonder, then, that William of Ockham in the fourteenth century had already taken such doctrines as the existence of God and transubstantiation out of the arena of philosophical theology and made them objects of implicit faith, that is, doctrines that are to be accepted simply on the word of the church.

There is little doubt that the young Calvin was trained in terminist philosophy, which is doubtless part of the "mire" from which he said God had to extricate him before he could confidently and joyfully understand that terms—specifically the terms of Scripture—genuinely stand for their objects.

Schooling at Orléans and Bourges

Around this time Calvin, because his father had concluded
that the legal profession would be more profitable for his
son, obediently stopped studying for the priesthood and
transferred to the University of Orléans where he began to
pursue his licentiate in civil law under Pierre de l'Estoile,
the leading law professor in France. Here he studied the
Corpus Iuris Civilis that was comprised of the following
three parts:

> Part One: Known as the *Codex*, this part was the authoritative
> statement of Roman law, dealing not only with church law, with
> chapters treating such topics as church buildings, bishops, baptism,
> heretics, images, and the Trinity, but also with civil law, with chapters
> dealing with such topics as the disposal of rain water, rights of
> way, leases, purchase and possession, marriage and divorce, and
> inheritance.
>
> Part Two: Called the *Digesta* (also known as the *Pandecta*),
> this part was a massive compilation of statements of early
> Roman jurists that provided a historical commentary on the
> *Codex*.
>
> Part Three: Named the *Institutiones*, this part was the
> elementary textbook for law-students.

Within a year Calvin so distinguished himself in the knowledge of law that he was no longer looked upon as a student
and was employed to teach classes in the absence of
professors for illness. The law faculty was prepared to
bestow upon him a doctorate of law free of charge at this
time but he declined to take it.

As an aspiring humanist scholar Calvin also learned and
studied Greek there with Melchior Wolmar, a man with
Lutheran leanings, who supplied Calvin with several of
Luther's works, namely, "The Liberty of the Christian Man"
in which Luther carefully laid out his doctrine of justification
by faith alone (particularly for Pope Leo X), his two

"Catechisms," and the Marburg Articles of 1529.[21] Calvin would later dedicate his commentary on 2 Corinthians to Wolmar. Calvin's cousin, Pierre Robert Olivétan (the last a nickname meaning "midnight oil" that friends had given him because of his late-night study habits), who had already become a Lutheran and who translated the Bible into French in 1532-35 also seems to have had no little influence on his thinking at this time and may well have been the primary human instrument used by God in bringing about his conversion.

Calvin left Orléans in 1529 or 1530 when around twenty years of age and began his study of law at the University of

---

[21]A word about the Marburg Articles is in order. In October 1529 a meeting took place in Marburg that would have a lasting negative effect on the young Protestant cause. At the invitation of Landgrave Philip of Hesse, Martin Luther and Ulrich Zwingli met for a Colloquy to discuss their Protestant differences. While they agreed on fourteen of fifteen articles that Luther himself had drawn up, they did not agree on the fifteenth: whether the real body and blood of Christ are physically present in, with, and under the bread and wine of the sacrament of the Lord's Supper. Luther said yes, Zwingli said no. Zwingli regarded this matter as a secondary issue which should not disrupt Christian unity, but Luther saw it as a fundamental article and said at this time to both the Strasbourg and Swiss delegations: "Your spirit is different from ours." Luther then refused to take Zwingli's hand as a sign of brotherhood, saying to the Swiss Reformer and his supporters: "You do not belong to the communion of the Christian Church. We cannot acknowledge you as brothers." The Swiss delegates nearly exploded at this insult but managed to control their tempers. The two delegations parted, and regrettably Protestantism remained divided because of Luther's unyielding insistence on his view of the Real Presence based upon his exegesis of Christ's words, "This is my body"—a division within the Protestant movement that Calvin would later struggle mightily, though unsuccessfully, throughout his professional career to overcome for the sake of the unity, strength, and witness of the Reformation cause.

Bourges under the renowned Italian law professor Andrea Alciati.[22]

Calvin then left Bourges and returned to Noyon in late May 1530 to oversee the burial of his father who had died excommunicate, having fallen out of favor with the church over a business matter. Then he lived for a short time in Paris in the Collège Fortet (yet another college of the University of Paris), pursued literary studies at the Collège Royale, and continued to study Latin and Greek under Pierre Danès and began the study of Hebrew under Francois Vatable. At some point in time, perhaps around late 1530, he returned to Orléans.[23] We know from legal documents that he had been awarded his Licentiate in Law by 1532. The Doctorate in Law, a title conferred automatically soon after the awarding of the licentiate degree, was probably granted shortly afterward but we do not know this for certain.

Free to pursue his own way after the death of his father, Calvin published his first (and only humanist) work around

---

[22]Calvin met there a ten-year old boy, born June 24, 1519, named Theodore Beza who was studying Greek under Melchior Wolmar (who had also recently transferred to Bourges). Beza, ten years Calvin's junior, would some day become Calvin's trusted successor at Geneva and his first biographer.

[23]Around this time in Calvin's life Ulrich Zwingli, leader of the German-speaking Swiss Reformation, was killed in the Swiss civil wars at Kappel on Oct. 11, 1531. Heinrich Bullinger (1504-75) succeeded him on December 9 as the leader of Zwinglianism in the city of Zürich. Readers may want to consult J. H. Merle d'Aubigne, *For God and His People: Ulrich Zwingli and the Swiss Reformation* (Greenville, SC: BJU, 2000); S. Simpson, *Life of Ulrich Zwingli, the Swiss Patriot and Reformer* (New York: Baker & Taylor, 1902); G. R. Potter, *Zwingli* (Cambridge: University Press, 1977); and *Zwingli and Bullinger*, edited by Geoffrey W. Bromiley (Library of Christian Classics; Philadelphia: Westminster, 1953), Volume 24, for more information on the lives and theologies of these two Reformers.

1532 at the age of twenty-three. It was a commentary on *De clementia* (*On Clemency*) by the younger Seneca, the Roman Stoic philosopher and Nero's counselor. Written in excellent Latin, Calvin quoted fifty-six Latin and twenty-two Greek writers, seven church fathers, as well as several humanists of his own day. It is interesting to observe that he made only three rather insignificant references to Bible passages: the first, to a king's wrath; the second, a passing reference to Romans 13 to the effect that "power comes from God alone, and those that exist have been ordained by God;" the third, to the duties of masters to servants.[24]

The book did not sell well even though Calvin was attempting in it to stand on the shoulders of Nero's old adviser and to give counsel to the kings of his own day—particularly to Francis I of France—as to how they should rule their people not only wisely and justly but also mercifully. At this point in his life evidence would indicate that Calvin was writing as a thinker of "the humanist circle which flirted with evangelism in Paris."[25]

CALVIN'S CONVERSION TO THE "NEW FAITH"

If in this respect 1532 was a year of disappointment for him, in another respect that year was to be the most momentous of his life. At Orléans he continued to study law and was

---

[24]For Ford Lewis Battles' analysis of Calvin's commentary on Seneca's *Two Books on Clemency*, see his "Introduction" to his translation of Calvin's *Institutes of the Christian Religion (1536 Edition)* (Revised edition; Grand Rapids: Eerdmans, 1986), xxii-xxiv. Battles suggests that this commentary, expressed in a "humanistic if not outright pagan tone" (xxiv), might be viewed as Calvin's "first apology to Francis I."

[25]Andrew Pettegree, "Reformation and Counter-Reformation," in *A World History of Christianity*, edited by Adrian Hastings (Grand Rapids: Eerdmans, 1999), 258.

given the office of Annual Deputy of the Dean for the Nation of Picardy in the University. So it seems fairly clear that Calvin was at this time in Orléans restlessly looking, wherever he could, for opportunities to continue his humanist education in the study of law. But he then experienced what he would later term his "unexpected [or "sudden"] conversion" from Romanism to Protestantism (more precisely, to soteric Lutheranism), the details of which conversion we know very little.

We know, of course, that he knew of Lefèvre's "Luther-esque" ideas; that he had listened to Melchior Wolmar, his Lutheran-leaning Greek teacher; that he had discussed Lutheranism with his cousin Olivétan; and that he had been reading Luther and Zwingli. But he mentions no human agency in the account of his conversion. All he says— tantalizingly little, by the way—about his actual conversion is the following, found in his "Preface" to his *Commentary on the Psalms*:

> I tried my best to work hard [in the study of law], yet God at last turned my course in another direction by the secret rein of his providence. What happened first, since I was too obstinately addicted to the superstitions of Popery to be easily extricated from so profound an abyss of mire, was that God by an unexpected [or "sudden"] conversion [*subita*²⁶ *conversione*] subdued and reduced my mind to a teachable frame. And so this taste of true godliness...set me on fire with such a desire to progress that I pursued the rest of my studies [in law] more cooly, although I did not give them up altogether.²⁷

---

²⁶According to Cottret, *Calvin: A Biography*, 68, A. Ganoczy in the interest of viewing Calvin's conversion as a gradual development, contended that the Latin *subita* "must be understood as...[indicating a conversion] 'suffered' (*subie* in French) by Calvin, and not an instantaneous conversion." Cottret disagrees, as do I.

It has often been suggested (rightly so, in my opinion) that we should also see an account of his conversion thinly veiled behind his "Protestant" layman in his "Reply to Sadoleto." I will say more about this later treatise in the next lecture.

CALVIN'S WINSOME WAY

We will conclude this first lecture after I address one final matter about Calvin's youth and young manhood. Adolf von Harnack (1851-1930), the Ritschlian church historian, perniciously described Calvin as "the man who never smiled." This is a very wrong assessment of Calvin's character. Calvin taught that

> laughter is the gift of God; and he held it [to be] the right, or rather the duty, of the Christian man to practice it in its due season. He is constantly joking with his friends in his letters, and he eagerly joins with them in all the joys of life. "I wish I were with you for half a day," he writes to one of them, "to laugh with you"...he enjoyed a joke hugely, with that open-mouthed laugh, which as one of his biographers phrases it, belonged to the men of the sixteenth century.[28]

We have every letter between Calvin and John Knox, Warfield notes, and in them Calvin is always seeking to make Knox "more human," not vice versa.

---

[27]See Williston Walker, *John Calvin: The Organiser of Reformed Protestantism* (New York: Schocken, 1906), chapter IV(reprinted 2005 by Christian Focus www.christianfocus.com); Ford Lewis Battles, "Introduction" to his translation of the 1536 edition of the *Institutes*, xxvi-xxxiv; and T.H.L. Parker, *John Calvin*, 192-6, all three of whom discuss the possible dates and human antecedents of Calvin's conversion.

[28]Warfield, "Calvin's Doctrine of the Creation," *The Works of Benjamin B. Warfield*, V, 297.

I cannot leave this issue without citing one more Calvin scholar, Émile Doumergue, a major Calvin biographer who wrote a seven-volume Calvin biography, who says of Calvin's magnetic character in his youth and young manhood:

Thus he journeys from place to place, from north to south and from south to north, through France and through the churches, seeing, hearing, observing, noting, enriching his heart and his conscience not less than his understanding with all that he encounters among men as well as in libraries; a prodigy of work, of rigorous self-denial, and yet full of youthfulness, highly esteemed, always welcomed. All circles dispute for him, and on all he exercises that mysterious power of seduction and attraction which is one of the most characteristic signs of the sovereignty of genius. All who know him love him; and those who love him cannot resist the wish, or let us say the necessity, of seeing him again. They leave, one after another — [in] *Noyon*: his brother, his sister, his successor in the chaplaincy..., his successor in the curacy...; — [in] *Paris*: his master Mathurin Cordier, his fellow pupils of the house of Montmor, his friends the Cops, his friends the Budés; — [in] *Orléans*: the sons of his friend Daniel; — [in] *Bourges*: the Colladins; — [in] *Angoulême*: his host himself who cannot be separated from him; — [in] *Poitiers* Véron, the *procureur* Babinot, the lecturer in the Institute, Saint-Vertumien: a strange enough procession, but one which attests the fascination exercised upon hearts by one whom men have dared to reproach with not being able to feel or inspire affection.[29]

We leave Calvin now as a brilliant young scholar, possessed of one of the most thoroughly trained legal minds of his time, taught by the best authorities in all Europe in all the subjects in which he was schooled, a man whose presence was much sought after by all who knew him. But more importantly, we leave him

---

[29]Émile Doumergue, *Jean Calvin. Les hommes et les choses de son temps* (Lausanne: Georges Bridel et Cie, 1899), 1, 515.

as a man converted from the false soteriology of Rome by the biblical soteriology of Wittenberg.

CHAPTER TWO

THE YOUNG REFORMER
AND HIS *INSTITUTES*

MORE ON CALVIN'S CONVERSION

In our first lecture we traced God's initial preparations of John Calvin for the great task to which he was calling him. We observed God's providential working in his life from his birth in 1509, through his acquisition of the best humanist education of the day at the Universities of Paris, Orléans, and Bourges, up to his conversion which occurred probably in the city of Orléans in 1532 or, less likely, in Paris in early or mid 1533, when around twenty-three years old.

As we noted earlier, Calvin tells us very little about what he termed his "unexpected [or "sudden"] conversion" from Catholicism to the "new faith" that was abroad in the land. I mentioned, you may recall, that we very likely have a thinly veiled description of it in his "Reply to Sadoleto," an essay that he wrote dated September 1, 1539.[1] The events lying behind the writing of this essay are as follows: After Calvin's expulsion from Geneva in 1538 (which expulsion we will discuss more fully at the end of this lecture), Jacopo Sadoleto of Carpentras in southern France, a Cardinal in the

---

[1]The argument of Fritz Büsser, *Calvins Urteil über sich selbst* (Zürich, 1950), 30-1, that Calvin's experience could not even "partially lie behind this account" because "it would be difficult to identify him with the layman" in Calvin's *Reply* does not really speak to the issue. The parallels to the Psalms "Preface" are great. For example, both refer to the early period. And Calvin has a layman speak because Sadoleto used a layman as his spokesman.

Roman Catholic Church, seized the moment and attempted to persuade the civil magistrates and citizenry of Protestant Geneva to return to "mother Church" by means of a letter written in fine Latin and dated March 18, 1539. He concluded his "Letter to the Genevans" by imagining a faithful Catholic layman and a Protestant layman standing before God in the final judgment to be examined for "right faith." He has the Catholic essentially say: "I was obedient to the Catholic Church." He has the Protestant acknowledge that, for all his good intentions, he has been "the author of great seditions and schism" in the church. Of course, Sadoleto has God approving of the Catholic because "the Church errs not" and "even if she did err..., no such error would be condemned in him who should, with a mind sincere and humble toward God, have followed the faith and authority of his ancestors."[2] And, of course, Sadoleto has God disapproving of the schismatic Protestant.[3]

---

[2]Jacopo Sadoleto, "Letter to the Genevans," *A Reformation Debate*, edited by John C. Olin (Grand Rapids: Baker, 1966), 45. Both Sadoleto's letter and Calvin's reply were originally published by Wendelin Rihel in Strasbourg in September 1539. Calvin's translation of both letters in French was published by Michel du Bois in Geneva in January 1540.

[3]The charge is often made today, as Sadoleto implied in his letter to the Genevans when he compared the church to the seamless garment of the Lord that even heathen soldiers were unwilling to divide, that there was only one church until the sixteenth century and then the Reformation destroyed the unity of the church with its many sects. Kurt Aland rightly rejoins in his *Four Reformers* (Minneapolis: Augsburg, 1979), 136-7, that the Christian church had already divided five hundred years before the Reformation into Eastern and Western churches when the papal legates laid Leo IX's bull of excommunication on the altar of the Hagia Sophia church in Constantinople on June 16, 1054, a division that continues to this day. And before that, in the fifth and sixth centuries, this alleged unified church that the Reformation is accused of splitting was divided when a number of churches separated

Calvin concluded his reply to Sadoleto by adroitly taking up the same device. His representation of the Protestant layman's answer before God makes for extremely interesting reading, and in it one very likely sees Calvin's description of his own conversion from Catholicism to Protestant Evangelicalism.[4] Let me give you in a greatly abbreviated form the description that he places in the mouth of his Protestant who is standing before God in judgment:

I, O Lord, as I had been educated from a boy, always professed the Christian faith. But at first I had no other reason for my faith than that which then everywhere prevailed...the rudiments in which I had been instructed were of a kind which could neither properly train me to the legitimate worship of your Deity, nor pave the way for me to a sure hope of salvation...the method of obtaining [salvation], which [my teachers] pointed out, was by making satisfaction to you for offenses....

When, however, I had performed all [the works of satisfaction they told me to perform]...I was still far-off from true peace of conscience; for, whenever I descended into myself, or raised my mind to you, extreme terror seized me—terror which no expiations or satisfactions [of mine] could cure...Still, as nothing better offered, I continued the course which I had begun, when, lo, a very different form of doctrine started up, not one which led us away from the Christian profession, but one which brought it back to its fountainhead, and, as it were, clearing away the dross, restored it to its original purity. Offended by [its] novelty, I lent an unwilling ear, and at first, I confess, strenuously and passionately resisted [it]; for...one thing in particular made me averse to those new teachers, viz., [my] reverence for the Church. But when I opened my ears, and allowed myself to be taught, I perceived that this

---

from the church over the issues of Nestorianism (fifth century) and Monophysitism (sixth century).

[4]John Calvin, "Reply to Sadoleto," *A Reformation Debate*, 86-90. See Ford Lewis Battles, "Introduction" to his translation of Calvin's 1536 edition of the *Institutes*, xxviii-xxxiv.

fear of derogating the majesty of the Church was groundless. For
they reminded me [of many of the church's errors by taking me to
the Scriptures]. They told me, moreover, as a means of pricking
my conscience, that I could not safely connive at these things as if
they concerned me not; that so far are you from patronizing any
voluntary error, that even he who is led astray by mere ignorance
does not err with impunity...My mind being now prepared for
serious attention, I at length perceived, as if light had broken in
upon me, in what a style of error I had wallowed, and how much
pollution and impurity I had thereby contracted. Being exceedingly
alarmed at the misery into which I had fallen, and much more at
that which threatened me in the view of eternal death, I...made it
my first business to betake myself to your way, condemning my
past life, not without groans and tears. And now, O Lord, what
remains to a wretch like me but, instead of defense, earnestly to
supplicate you not to judge according to its deserts that fearful
abandonment of your Word, from which, in your wondrous
goodness, you have at last delivered me.[5]

This, as I said, is quite likely Calvin's description of his own
conversion experience in 1532.

Whatever one may finally conclude in this regard, we left
Calvin in our first lecture, as we said then, as a brilliant young
scholar, one of the most thoroughly trained scholars of his
time, taught by the best minds in all Europe in all the subjects
in which he was schooled, a serious man whose presence
was much sought after by all who knew him. But more
importantly, we left him as a converted man. Now we want
to continue our coverage of his life by tracing the life of the
young reformer from his conversion in Orléans in 1532 up
to and including his first period of ministry at Geneva that
ended in 1538, a period of six years.

---

[5]Calvin, "Reply to Sadoleto," *A Reformation Debate*, 87-90. I have
employed modern pronouns in this quotation rather than the old English
pronouns that appear in this edition's translation.

CALVIN ON THE RUN

After his conversion in 1532, in 1533 Calvin returned to Paris from Orléans and took up residency again at the Collège Fortet. Immediately he threw in his lot with the Reformation cause and at secret meetings of French "Lutherans" he was often called upon (much to his surprise, he says) to teach them the Bible.

He almost certainly assisted also in the writing, at his friend Nicholas Cop's request, of Cop's inaugural address as the newly elected Rector of the University of Paris, which Cop delivered on November 1 of that year at the Church of the Cordeliers before the four faculties (theology, law, medicine, and arts) of the university.[6] It was a plea of impulsive enthusiasm for a reformation of the church more in line with Jacques Lefèvre's Angoulême supporters than with the New Testament gospel. Nevertheless, it was a bold attack on the scholastic theologians of the day who were represented as ignorant of the gospel as Cop understood it, many of whom sat before him in his audience. Permit me to give you a short sample of that plea:

> This is the difficulty those most wretched Sophists [*Sophistae*, that is, the Sorbonne theologians] have run into; they argue interminably over goat's wool, they quarrel, they dispute, they

---

[6]Scholars debate whether Calvin had any part in the writing of Cop's address. Discovering a fragment of the text in Calvin's hand among his deceased friend's papers, Theodore Beza in 1575 hesitantly attributed to Calvin a part in writing it. There are a number of significant parallels in it with Calvin's later writings. And if he did not contribute to its writing, one wonders why Calvin would have felt the need to flee Paris later in the month, along with Cop, when the authorities sought to arrest Cop. We do know that the authorities ransacked Calvin's room at the Collège du Fortet, confiscated his papers, and seized his correspondence.

discuss (but nothing about faith, nothing about the love of God, nothing about the forgiveness of sins, nothing about grace, nothing about justification, nothing about true works). Or if they do discuss rightly, they vilify and contaminate everything, and enclose it within their own sophistical laws. I beg of you all here present never to sit back and accept these heresies, these insults against God.[7]

The Sorbonne—the theological faculty of the University of Paris—regarded this oration of their new Rector a "Lutheran" manifesto of war against the Catholic Church and condemned Cop's address to the flames. Sometime before November 26 of that same year Cop, hearing that the authorities were about to arrest him, fled from Paris and escaped to Basel. The authorities also looked for Calvin who escaped as well, one tradition saying that he went through a back room window and, dressed as a vinedresser with a hoe over his shoulder, made his way to Noyon.

In early 1534 Calvin traveled to Angoulême and lived with a friend, Louis du Tillet, a canon of Angoulême whose father was a wealthy nobleman, under the assumed name of Charles d'Espeville and also under the protection of Queen Marguerite of Navarre who was both a Lutheran sympathizer and sister of King Francis I (France's absolute monarch who reigned from 1515 to 1547). Many people came to Angoulême seeking instruction from this hunted man, again to his surprise. And it was there in Angoulême, in the library that the du Tillet family made available to him, he probably began to write his *Institutes of the Christian Religion*.

In April 1534 Calvin journeyed to Nérac and there met for the first time (and spent some time with) Jacques Lefèvre, the church reformer we mentioned in our first lecture who never broke from the Roman church but who had published

---

[7]For the full text of Cop's address one may consult Battles' translation of it in his translation of the 1536 edition of the *Institutes* (Grand Rapids: Eerdmans, 1975), 363-72, especially 365-6.

in 1512 a commentary on Paul's letters in which he advanced some "Lutheresque" ideas and in 1523 his own translation of the New Testament. At this time (1534) Lefèvre was about a hundred years old. Those scholars who put Calvin's conversion as late as this year suggest that his time with Lefèvre was directly instrumental in bringing Calvin to his Protestant faith. But he was almost certainly already a converted "Lutheran" by 1532. I would suggest that if he gained anything from this meeting he probably concluded that men such as Lefèvre who were trying to reform the church from within were destined to fail, for we see him soon taking action to leave the Roman church altogether.

Also in 1534 Calvin, when around twenty-five years old and probably while still in Angoulême, wrote his first theological book, *De Psychopannychia* (*On the Sleep of the Soul*), in which he refuted the contention of some emerging (Anabaptist?) groups that the soul sleeps between death and the resurrection.[8] However, it was not published until 1542. (After some revision Calvin republished it in Strasbourg in 1545 and finally came out with a French translation in 1558 at the request of William Farel.)

Approaching twenty-five years of age now, which was the normal time for ordination to the priesthood, Calvin journeyed to Noyon and summarily resigned his church benefices on May 4, 1534 and thus closed all formal connections with the Roman Catholic Church. Because the Noyon archives record that a *Jean Cauvin* had been jailed

---

[8]One may find this neglected work in *Selected Works of John Calvin: Tracts and Letters*, edited by Henry Beveridge and Jules Bonnet (Reprint; Grand Rapids: Baker, 1983), 3, 413-90. For Battles' discussion of *Psychopannychia* see the "Introduction" to his translation of the 1536 edition of the *Institutes*, xl-xliii. For another discussion of it see Bernard Cottret, *Calvin: A Biography*, translated by M. Wallace McDonald (Grand Rapids: Eerdmans, 2000), 77-82.

for a church disturbance on May 26, some scholars opine that apparently Calvin had shown dissatisfaction in some manner with the church service there and was jailed for a short time but was released unharmed. Other scholars suggest that this was another John Calvin, for the archives indicate that the jailed man possessed an alias—*Jean Cauvin dict Mudit*. If they are right, it would appear that the latter John Calvin did not want to be identified with the former!

After this trip to Noyon he returned to Paris, now with no source of income, lodging with his friend, a Protestant merchant named Etienne de la Forge who would soon be martyred, on his way back to Angoulême.

Toward the end of 1534 he left Angoulême and slipped into Paris again. There he met for the first time the Spanish physician, Michael Servetus, who had just published his book, *On the Errors of the Trinity*. Servetus challenged Calvin to a debate, and Calvin, accepting Servetus' challenge at the risk of his own safety, appeared at the arranged debate site but Servetus never showed. Calvin later sent him a copy of his *Institutes* and urged him to reconsider his views, and twenty years later he reminded Servetus of that aborted meeting during his trial at Geneva: "You know that at that time I was ready to do everything for you, and did not even count my life too dear that I might convert you from your errors." Would that he had succeeded but in God's mysterious providence it was not to be!

THE "PLACARD INCIDENT"

In November 1534 a terrible persecution of Protestants began in Paris as the result of what has come to be called the "Placard Incident" directed against the Mass, the heart of the Roman Catholic system. Antoine Marcourt, a noted pamphleteering pastor from Neuchâtel, had placards, thirty-seven centimeters by twenty-five and printed in Gothic characters, posted on October 17 in many places, including Paris, Orléans, Amboise, and even Blois, on the bedroom door of King Francis I, which act infuriated the king. Due providentially to the discovery in 1943 in Berne, Switzerland of strips of the original placards that were being used in the binding of a sixteenth-century book, we can now read for the first time in over four hundred years the authentic text of this important historical document.[9]

Its Negative Impact on French Evangelicals

While what these placards said about the Mass is, in my opinion, true enough,[10] this acerbic incident resulted in an

---

[9]For the full text of the placards one may consult Battles' translation of it in his translation of the 1536 edition of the *Institutes*, 339-42.

[10]The placards stressed the sole priesthood of Christ who by his unique sacrifice rendered the priesthood of men and the Roman Catholic Mass in particular forever unnecessary. Marcourt under-scored that Christ had offered himself up "once and for all" (χτδ°;ν°, Rom 6:10; Heb 7:27; 9:12, 25-26 [°Ψν°], 28 [°Ψν°]; 10:10-14). The Mass, Marcourt affirmed, is an absurd proceeding, full of "bell-ringing, cries, chantings, ceremonies, candlelightings, censings, disguises, and other sorts of buffoonery, by which the poor world is like a flock of sheep miserably deceived, and by these ravening wolves eaten, gnawed, and devoured." And the Roman Catholic priests "kill, burn, destroy, murder as brigands all those who have contradicted them, for anything else than force they do not have."

These placards, notes Cottret in his *Calvin: A Biography*, 83, made the Letter to the Hebrews "even more than Romans...the cornerstone of the French Reformation":

In the space of one night an invisible frontier cut across the [French] kingdom.... Neither justification by faith, nor the role of the Word, nor the predominance of Scripture had constituted [in France] a clear line of demarcation between [Rome and the Reformation]. But the Mass—behold the watershed that henceforth divided two confessions. Between October 17 and 18 "a dream dissolved," that of a unity henceforth lost.

outbreak of persecution, approved by King Francis I, against the French Evangelicals,[11] many of them being fined and/or imprisoned, many having their tongues slit, many being tortured in the whipping gallows, and many being burned alive slowly over fire. As we shall see shortly, this persecution had at least one salutary effect: it provoked Calvin to publish in 1536, sooner that he would have otherwise wished, the first edition of his *Institutes* in defense of his persecuted French brothers and sisters.

The following year, 1535, Calvin left Angoulême and traveled to Basel[12] and lived there about a year under the assumed name of Martin Lucanius (an altered spelling of Calvin) to escape the persecution of the Evangelicals in his native land. While there he wrote for Pierre Robert Olivétan, his twenty-nine-year-old cousin, the Latin preface to Olivétan's French translation of the entire Bible.[13] Calvin supervised the revision of this translation in 1536, 1538, 1539, 1540, and in 1543, and continued the work of perfecting its accuracy and its French in 1546 and 1551. His labor, with the assistance of Theodore Beza and Louis Budé, finally produced the French "Geneva Bible," published by Robert Estienne in Geneva in 1553, that dominated French-speaking Protestantism for two centuries.

---

[11]Guillaume Budé was a major antagonist against the French Evangelicals. In his *De transitu Hellenismi ad Christianismum* (March 1535) he condemned the Protestant Reformation as populist and an "abominable crime committed by madmen" (Cottret, *Calvin*, 85).

[12]The work of reforming the church in Basel had been chiefly that of Johannes Oecolampadius (d. 1531) who was succeeded by Oswald Myconius.

[13]For the full text of Calvin's Latin Preface to Olivétan's translation, one may consult Battles' translation of the 1536 edition of the *Institutes*, 373-77. Cottret provides a very useful discussion of Olivétan's French translation in his *Calvin: A Biography*, 97-101.

There in Basel Calvin also continued working on the first edition of his *Institutes*.

Its Pro-Active Effect on Calvin

Because the Protestant princes of Germany—whose good will Francis I needed in his rivalries with young Charles I of Spain who in 1519 had been elected emperor of the Holy Roman Empire, henceforth to be known as Charles V—were beginning to view with extreme disfavor the persecution of the Protestants that Francis I was allowing to go on in his country, the king of France felt it necessary to issue a public letter on February 1, 1535 in which he charged the Protestants of France with anarchistic aims designed for the "overthrow of all things." The tone of his letter suggested that there was a vast difference between the sober, orderly German Protestants and the so-called "radical" French Protestants. His explanation demanded a response but from whom? In the "Preface" to his *Commentary on the Psalms* Calvin wrote some twenty-two years later:

> Seeing this was done by the tricksters of the [French] Court, I felt that my silence would be treachery and that I should oppose [this letter] with all my might not only lest the undeserved shedding of innocent blood of holy martyrs should be concealed with false report, but also lest they [the persecutors] should go on in [the] future to whatever slaughter they pleased without arousing the pity of any. These were my reasons for publishing the *Institutes:* first, that I might vindicate from unjust affront my brethren whose death was precious in the sight of the Lord; and, second, that some sorrow and anxiety should move foreign peoples [to respond], since the same suffering threatened many [of them].

THE 1536 EDITION OF THE *INSTITUTES*

Having received word that some of his friends in Paris—de la Forge, Milon, Du Bourg, Poille—had died in the flames,

Calvin, being then only twenty-six years old, put everything else aside and completed and published in March 1536 in the city of Basel the first edition of his *Institutes*, writing a dedicatory Preface to King Francis I who was permitting and by his February 1, 1535 letter actually justifying the Roman Church's cruel persecution of his Protestant subjects. In his Preface, published with every subsequent edition of the *Institutes*, he called upon the king to investigate and to stop the unjust persecution of the Evangelicals. Calvin's *Institutes* is placed, therefore, in a "political framework," as it were, beginning with his letter to the French king and ending with his famous chapter on civil government (4.20).

It is important to note several things about this Preface. First, in it Calvin is *not* asking the king for mercy or for toleration of the Evangelicals. As a trained lawyer he is asking the king for *justice*: "I *demand justly* that you take up the whole knowledge of this case." Second, he is not arguing in it that there should be room for more than one church in a realm. His claim here is that the Evangelical Protestants are the legitimate heirs of the New Testament faith and therefore they represent the one true, holy, catholic, and apostolic church, and that it is the Roman Catholic Church that has deserted the New Testament faith. In sum, the heart of the matter that Calvin wants the king to face is this: Who can rightly claim to represent the one true, holy, catholic, and apostolic church? Rome or the Evangelical Protestants? Third, to undergird the Evangelical claim he takes up and refutes one by one the Romanist charges against the Evangelical doctrine:

- "Their doctrine is new," says Rome, to which Calvin responds: "Our doctrine is not a novelty to the New Testament; it is a novelty only to the Romanist who forsook it years ago."

- "Their doctrine is unknown," says Rome, to which Calvin responds: "Our doctrine is not unknown to the New Testament; it is unknown to the Romanist whose fault it is that it has lain so long unknown and buried."

- "Their doctrine is uncertain," says Rome, to which Calvin responds: "Our doctrine is not uncertain; we are so sure of its truthfulness that we fear neither the terrors of death nor God's judgment seat."

- "Their doctrine lacks authenticating miracles," says Rome, to which Calvin responds: "We have our authenticating miracles, even the miracles of the New Testament that attest to the gospel taught by the Apostles and the same gospel that we preach. Rome, having a new and different doctrine from that of the New Testament, requires new and different miracles. Moreover, Rome's miracles are counterfeit miracles originating from the Devil."

Fourth, actually citing them, he shows that the church fathers do not support Romanist teaching and practice but support rather the Evangelical doctrine. Fifth, he shows that Rome's appeal to custom is an appeal against biblical truth. Sixth, he shows that Rome's representation of the nature of the church is erroneous because it lacks the marks of the true church, even "the pure preaching of God's Word and the lawful administration of the sacraments." Here he also turns Rome's own papal history against its claim that the Roman pontiff represents in himself and not in any council the church by noting that the Council of Basel (1431-49), lawfully convened not by one but by two popes (Pope Martin V and his successor, Pope Eugenius IV), deposed Eugenius on June 25, 1439 for schism, rebellion, and obstinacy, along with all the cardinals and bishops who had acted with him in the dissolution of the council, and elected in his stead Amadeus VIII, Duke of Savoy, who took office on January 1, 1440 as Pope Felix V. When Eugenius curried the favor and won the support of the new Emperor Frederick III, Felix issued a bull anathematizing Eugenius. But through political intrigue and unkept promises by Eugenius to recognize the superiority of general councils, he was able to retain his hold on the Roman see. Consequently, Felix revoked his anathema and abdicated his papal throne in exchange for a cardinal's cap, and Eugenius claimed the papal throne again. Where then, Calvin asks, resides the church? In a recalcitrant, dishonest pope judged schismatic by a duly-convened church council and from whose heretical party "have come forth all future popes, cardinals, bishops, abbots, and priests," or in the church council that "was general, which lacked nothing of outward majesty, was solemnly convoked by two [papal] bulls, consecrated by the presiding legate of the Roman see, well ordered in every respect, and preserving the same dignity to the end?"[14] Seventh, he shows that Rome's charge that the present tumults in the land are directly traceable to evangelical preaching is false; they are to be traced rather to Anabaptist and other radical practices. Finally, he

---

[14]Implicit in Calvin's question is the unique quandary that Rome has wrestled with for centuries, namely, where its ultimate authority resides. If Rome answers, "In church councils," then it must admit that its claim respecting the ultimacy of papal authority is erroneous. Therefore, it will not admit the ultimacy of church councils. If Rome answers, "In the pope," then it must admit that in this case one of its duly convened general church councils erred, which it does not want to admit either. Since both attitudes are part of Rome's "second authority" alongside the authority of Scripture, namely, its tradition that has often erred, Calvin would urge that better it would be if Rome, with Protestantism, would enthrone the Scriptures of the Old and New Testaments as the church's ultimate authority. This, of course, it will never do either.

admonishes the king to beware of acting on false charges, for the charge of sedition against the Evangelicals, he argues, is utterly false; they in fact live quiet, simple lives and pray for the king. He reminds the king that France already has laws and legal penalties sufficient to restrain the tumults that have arisen, and he concludes that if his appeal does not move the king to change his attitude toward the Evangelicals they will still trust the King of kings "to deliver the poor from their affliction and also to punish their despisers."

We do not know whether the king ever read Calvin's dedication, much less the *Institutes*, but we do know that Francis had already taken steps to cultivate the German Protestants as possible allies in the war with Charles V that was to break out early in 1536, by issuing on July 16, 1535 the Edict of Coucy that permitted those charged with heresy who had fled from France to return, provided they would desist from their errors and recant them within six months, and we know that by May 31, 1536, these "so-called" privileges were confirmed.

In any event, with the publication in 1536 of Calvin's *Institutes* for the first time someone had set down in writing for hard-pressed French Evangelicals the essential truths of the Reformation. Williston Walker, professor of church history at Yale University, says of the 1536 edition:

> ...it was not merely a handbook of theology which marked its young author as the ablest interpreter of Christian doctrine that the Reformation age had produced, but it was prefaced by a bold yet dignified and respectful Letter addressed to King Francis which at once placed Calvin at the head of French reformers and revealed him in the highest degree as a man of leadership.[15]

In another context Walker writes of this edition:

---

[15]Williston Walker, *John Calvin*, 128.

Though greatly to be enlarged and improved in the later editions on which he was unweariedly to labour till within five years of the close of his life, it stood forth, even in this early form, not merely as by far the most significant treatise that the reformers of France had yet produced, but without a superior as a clear, logical, and popularly apprehensible presentation of those principles for which all Protestantism contended. It was far more than a theoretical exposition of the Christian faith. Though in form not strictly a programme for action, it could easily yield the basis of a new constitution for the Church, and of a regulation of the moral life of the community. The felicity of its style, the logical cogency of argument, the precision of statement, which marked the volume were Calvin's own. The moral enthusiasm which shines through it was a kindling force. As a treatment of Christian doctrine, it was fresh and original. But it was even more a carefully wrought-out exposition of the Christian life, novel and inspiring in its clearness and earnestness.[16]

And Bernard Cottret states about the 1536 edition:

...the *Institutes* crossed "a historical threshold" It put "an end to the period of Lutheranizing, mysticizing, and evangelical wanderings" and furnished those who doubted the established church with "a body of precise dogmatic definitions."[17]

The *Institutes'* first edition had six chapters of some five hundred and twenty pages in which Calvin dealt with the following topics:

1. The Law of God
Calvin argues here that the whole human race has become totally corrupt and justly exposed to God's wrath. Hence any human effort to merit righteousness is unavailing; but

[16]Williston Walker, *John Calvin*, 145-46.
[17]Bernard Cottret, *Calvin: A Biography*, 112.

God forgives sins and gives a new heart to humble penitents who accept his gifts with "certain faith." The Law, therefore, is not man's rule of salvation, but a "looking glass" showing our condition. He then discusses the Ten Commandments and argues that the Law has three main uses: to restrain sinful mankind in the civil realm, to convict sinners and show them their need for Christ, and to provide a guide for Christian conduct.

2. Faith
Here Calvin distinguishes between intellectual recognition of God's existence and the truth of Scripture as narrative, on the one hand, over against belief on the other that places "all hope and confidence in God and Christ," the basis of this hope and confidence being Holy Scripture alone. He then treats the Trinity and proceeds to explain the Apostles' Creed.

3. Prayer
Here Calvin argues that prayer is to be offered to God in the name of Christ alone, not to or through saints. He then proceeds to an exposition of the Lord's Prayer.

4. The Sacraments of Baptism and the Lord's Supper
Calvin defines a sacrament as an "external sign by which the Lord sets forth and attests his goodwill toward us in order to sustain the weakness of our faith." The sacraments, he argues, require and witness to the preceding divine promise, like seals valueless in themselves that confirm that to which they are attached. He argues here for only two sacraments, both serving to strengthen our faith in God's remission of our sins and as a confession of him before men. He discusses the controversy between the Lutherans and Zwinglians over the nature of Christ's presence in the Lord's Supper and rejects both views: "...the sacrament is something spiritual,"

he writes. Since a physical body can be in but one place, Christ is "truly and efficaciously" but not locally present in the elements. He then goes on to reject the Roman mass in most energetic terms and urges that communion should be observed in a simple ritual at least once a week.

5. False Sacraments

Calvin vigorously argues that Rome's sacraments of Confirmation, Penance, Extreme Unction, Orders, and Marriage lack all the conditions a sacrament requires in order to be a sacrament: God's creating it, his giving the promise to which it is the witness, and his revealing it in Scripture. In connection with Penance, he criticizes in turn auricular confession to a priest, Rome's claim to possess a treasury of merit, papal indulgences, and the existence of purgatory. In connection with the so-called sacrament of Holy Orders, he contends that Holy Scripture "recognizes no other minister of the church than a preacher of the Word of God, called to govern the church, whom it calls now bishop, now a presbyter, and occasionally a pastor."

6. Christian Liberty, Ecclesiastical Power, and Civil Administration

Calvin argues here that the Christian enjoys a freedom that is above the Law viewed as a "test" of obedience though it remains an admonishing and stimulating influence: "[Christian] consciences," he writes, "submit to the Law not as if compelled by the force of the Law, but free from the yoke of the Law itself, they obey the will of God voluntarily." In sum, the Law is the Christian's rule of life. Christians are also free, he writes, in the use of "indifferent things": "Nor is it forbidden to laugh, or to enjoy food, or to add new possessions to old and ancestral property, or to be delighted with musical harmonies, or to drink wine," all showing that Calvin was anything but an ascetic.

For his guidance man is placed in this world under two governments, the spiritual and the temporal. The spiritual government has only one King, Christ, and one Law, the Scriptures. Its officers are "ministers" of the Word who have no right to add to or to subtract from the prescriptions contained therein. Because the function of the pastor and other church officers is laid out by the Word of God alone, Calvin finds no authority in the decrees of church councils or in the promulgations of the church fathers and bishops, save only as they are in agreement with the one standard of the written Word of God.

The temporal or civil government, he writes, has been established by God "to order our life for the society of men, to conform our conduct to civil justice, to reconcile us one with another, to nourish and preserve common peace and tranquility." The magistrate's duty is both to see that "public peace be not disturbed, and each safely possess his own," and to guard lest "idolatry, sacrilege against the name of God, blasphemies against his truth, or public offences against religion should break out or be spread among the people." To the magistrate, even to a magistrate of vicious and tyrannical character, full obedience is due, except where his command contradicts the revealed will of God. Then, he is to be respectfully disobeyed.[18]

Between the first three and the last three chapters a decidedly different writing style and atmosphere are discernable, the earlier chapters being less polemic and more calm, the last chapters being much more heated and controversial in tone. Many Calvin scholars have surmised from this that the

---

[18]For a fuller overview of the content of the first edition of the *Institutes* see Williston Walker, *John Calvin*, 136-45. For Battles' analysis of the six chapters of the first edition one may consult his "Introduction" to his translation of the 1536 edition of the *Institutes*, xlviii-lix.

last chapters were written after Calvin had heard of the 1534 martyrdoms of his friends and with rising indignation had determined that their names had to be defended. Hence he modified his earlier plan of a peacefully worked-out book on Christian doctrine. Now he apparently felt that he had to begin, as he himself said, to write as a lawyer or an apologist to defend his persecuted friends' reputations and their mutually held Evangelical cause.

CALVIN COMES TO GENEVA

That same year (1536) Calvin left Basel and traveled to Italy with Louis du Tillet, his wealthy friend from Angoulême, accompanying him. He spent six or eight weeks in Ferrara in the home of the sympathetic Duchess Renée (to whom he dictated from his deathbed in 1564 his last letter in French), daughter of King Louis XII of France, wife of the son of Lucrezia Borgia, and sister-in-law of Francis I. He tried to solicit her influence with her brother-in-law on behalf of the cause of the persecuted Protestants in France. Apparently she was unable to help, for she herself was eventually imprisoned for her Protestant faith, and her children were taken from her and reared by strangers in the Catholic faith. Calvin then made his way back to Basel, where Louis du Tillet left him (and returned not only home to Angoulême but also eventually back to the Catholic church[19]). Calvin then returned to Paris for a brief visit at which time he gave power of attorney privileges on June 2, 1536 to his brother Antoine regarding the sale of their parents' land in Noyon.

---

[19]Du Tillet apparently did not renounce the doctrine of justification by faith or the need for church reform but thought reform should be accomplished within and not apart from the church. Moreover, in his continuing correspondence with Calvin he expressed serious doubt that God had called Calvin to his vocation.

From Paris, with his brother Antoine and a half-sister accompanying him, Calvin started for Strasbourg in July 1536 in order to begin a scholar's life there, but because of the war that was raging between Francis I and Charles V he made a long detour south and stopped in Geneva on August 5, planning to spend only one night there on his way north to Strasbourg. This night was to prove to be a defining moment in his life. The year before, on November 29, 1535, the Genevan citizenry had revolted against its Catholic bishop and his supporter, the Duke of Savoy, and had become a Protestant city, mainly as the result of William Farel's preaching, though it then became largely dependent for a decade or more for protection upon the domineering Swiss Protestant cities of Berne and Zürich that were a beacon of evangelical reform.

William Farel

William Farel, sometimes called "the Elijah of the French Reformation," a bombastic, acidic, but fearlessly courageous preacher of Reformation ideas who had little talent for organization, had come to Geneva in October 1532 and December 1533 and had, with the help of Peter Viret, fostered the work of the Reformation there.[20] The night Calvin arrived in Geneva Farel, twenty years Calvin's senior, was informed that the young author of the *Institutes* was staying in the city and he called upon him and exhorted him to remain in Geneva to help him as a teacher and pastor. When Calvin protested that he was a scholar fit only for the writer's desk, Farel threatened him with the curse of Almighty God if he preferred the scholar's life of study to the work and cause of Christ in Geneva. Terrified by Farel's

---

[20]For an overview of Geneva's move from Catholicism to Protestantism that had become official on August 10, 1535 see John C. Olin, "Introduction" in *A Reformation Debate*, 13-15.

words, Calvin later wrote that he "felt as if God from on high had stretched out his hand to arrest me." So he submitted and accepted Farel's call to assist him in the ministry in the church of Geneva.

After a brief trip back to Basel to collect his few possessions Calvin returned to Geneva and began his labors there in September 1536, at first serving simply in the role of "Reader in Holy Scripture" and beginning what church historians designate as his "first Geneva period" which spanned September 1536 to April 1538—serving without pay, by the way, until the following February. The minutes of the city's Little Council refer to him at this time simply as *ille Gallus*—"that Frenchman."[21]

Geneva's Governmental Structure

Since I have referred to Geneva's "Little Council," a brief word about Geneva's government structure at this juncture may be helpful. At the head of the city's government was the twenty-five-man Little Council, composed of the four powerful magistrates or mayors known as Syndics, the city treasurer, and twenty others. The Council of the Two Hundred, established in 1527 and elected by the Little Council, somewhat strangely elected in turn those sitting on the Little Council. Between these two Councils was the rather useless Council of the Sixty that was little more than a holdover from the fourteenth century and whose function was mainly diplomatic, each member of which was also a member of the Council of the Two Hundred. Any business

---

[21]As far as we know Calvin was never ordained to the teaching ministry of the church in the sense that a duly-authorized body of elders laid hands on him and set him apart for the ministry. This may—or may not—have been done at some point in time. We simply have no record of such an ordination. We do know that Farel, and later Bucer, called him to involve himself in the work of their ministries.

went first to the Little Council, then to the Council of the Two Hundred. A fourth council—the General Council composed of all the heads of households in Geneva—played a more and more tenuous role; in Calvin's time it met twice annually: in February to elect the four Syndics and in November to set corn and wine prices. This arrangement appears to be somewhat cumbersome, but the Little Council members, sitting three times a week, actually wielded the executive or greatest power and in fact ran the city government. So, in sum, that was the magisterial system with which Calvin worked throughout his years at Geneva.

THE LAUSANNE DISPUTATION

An incident occurred in October 1536 that illustrates the young Calvin's great learning. The city of Lausanne was facing a vote by its citizenry regarding whether it would remain a Roman Catholic city or become a Protestant city. A debate, known by church historians as the Lausanne Disputation, was convened in the Lausanne Cathedral of Notre-Dame to assist in determining the matter. William Farel, who was to lead the Protestant cause, took "that Frenchman" with him. About one hundred and seventy-five Roman Catholic priests were in attendance. The debate focused on ten theses drawn up primarily by Peter Viret (1511-71), the Reformer of the Vaud region.[22] For the first three days of the disputations Calvin sat in silence and listened, much to Farel's chagrin. On the fourth day (October 5) the topic for debate turned to Thesis Three and its state-ment that Christ "withdrew from us in corporeal presence." Mimard, a Roman Catholic priest, began by

---

[22]The reader can find these ten theses in "The Lausanne Articles," *Calvin: Theological Treatises*, edited by J. K. S. Reid (Library of Christian Classics; Philadelphia: Westminster, 1954), XXII, 35-7.

reading a carefully prepared speech in which he accused the Reformers of holding in low esteem the teachings of Augustine and other early Fathers on the physical presence of the Lord in the Lord's Supper because they feared their authority that, he said, was against them. Suddenly, Calvin rose to his feet. All eyes turned toward him. He began to speak—without notes (and I condense here):

> …the reproach which you have made concerning the holy doctors of antiquity constrains me to say one word to remonstrate briefly how wrongly and groundlessly you accuse us in this connection. [He then begins to paraphrase the early Fathers from memory.] Cyprian speaking of the present matter that now occupies us in Book 2 of the Letters, Letter 3, says [he then paraphrases Cyprian]. Tertullian, refuting the error of Marcion, said [he then paraphrases Tertullian]. The author of the unfinished commentaries on Matthew that are attributed to St. John Chrysostom, in the eleventh homily, about in the middle, said [he then paraphrases this source]. Augustine in Epistle 23, very near the end, said [he then paraphrases Augustine]. In the book *Against Adimantus*, about the middle, Augustine declares [he again paraphrases Augustine]. At the beginning of [Augustine's] Homily on the Gospel on John, about the 8th or 9th section, he declares: "While this age endures, it is necessary that the Savior be on high…his body which ascended into heaven [is] in one place…." How will you then reconcile the view that the body appears on all the altars, is enclosed in all the little boxes, is every day and at the same time in a hundred places…? In the book *De fide ad Petrum Diaconum*, chapter 19, Augustine says [he then paraphrases this source]. In the epistle *ad Dardanum* Augustine testifies [he then paraphrases this source]. The whole world is easily able to understand with what audacity you reproach us with being contrary to the ancient doctors. Certainly if you had seen some of their pages, you would not have been so foolhardy as to pass such judgment as you have done, not even having seen the evidence. I advise and beseech you to charge us no longer with contradicting the ancient doctors in this matter with whom we are in fact in such accord.[23]

He sat down. The cathedral was silent. Then Jean Tandy, a Franciscan friar, stood and spoke:

> It seems to me that the sin against the Spirit that the Scriptures speak of is the stubbornness which rebels against manifest truth. In accordance with that which I have just heard, I confess to be guilty. Because of ignorance I have lived in error and I have spread the wrong teaching. I ask God's pardon for everything I have said and done against his honor; and ask the pardon of all of you people for the offense which I gave with my preaching up until now. I defrock myself henceforth to follow Christ and his pure doctrine alone....

Lausanne proceeded to vote to become a Protestant city, and day after day more and more Catholic priests—Mimard among them—declared themselves for the Protestant faith! The discourse of *ille Gallus* helped turn the tide, a living example of the power of truth when that truth is known and publicly expressed. The gracious God had vindicated his servant's obedient decision to come to the work in Geneva!

CALVIN'S DISMISSAL FROM GENEVA

Back in Geneva Calvin wrote three documents for the city of Geneva: the *Confession of Faith of 1536*, a *Catechism of the Church at Geneva* for instructing children, and his *Articles on the Organization of the Church and its Worship at Geneva*.[24]

Calvin was a stranger to Geneva's "byzantine factional politics," and as we shall see in a moment it was the

---

[23]The reader can find Calvin's impromptu Lausanne discourse in *Calvin: Theological Treatises*, 38-45.

[24]The reader can find the *Articles on the Organization of the Church and Its Worship at Geneva* in *Calvin: Theological Treatises*, 48-55.

provisions in the *Articles* pertaining to church discipline that eventually proved to be the "sticking point" for Geneva's Little Council and the Council of Two Hundred. The *Articles* affirmed that the pastors should have the right of *independent* exercise of ecclesiastical discipline in the church that up to this time was largely the creation of the civil magistracy and over which the civil magistracy exercised control.

In 1537 the Council of Two Hundred ordered all the citizens of the city to assent to Calvin's *Confession* and moved to banish those who would not take the oath. (As it turned out, the number of citizens who refused either to take the oath or to leave Geneva was so large that no one could compel them to leave.) Early in the following year, when Calvin argued before the Geneva magistrates that unworthy persons should not be permitted to partake of the Lord's Supper and that the ministers of the church should have the right to determine who would be given communion and the right to excommunicate the impenitent in the church, he was outmaneuvered by his opponents on the Council, and his efforts to introduce an independent ecclesiastical excommunication were effectively brought to an end on January 4 when the Council of Two Hundred voted "that the Supper should be refused to no one" and that the civil magistracy reserved to itself the admonishing of the erring and particularly the imposition of the penalty of excommunication.

Later, when Berne, the powerful German-speaking Protestant city, desirous of uniting the French-speaking Protestant cities proposed that the other Swiss Protestant cities conform their ceremonial practices to Bernese ceremonial practices and notified the Genevan government that they were considering calling a synod in Zürich to discuss this issue, the Little Council did not wait for the synod to meet but on March 11, 1538 approved the introduction of the Bernese ceremonies at Geneva. The Council then asked Calvin and Farel whether they would observe the

Bernese ceremonies or not. Both refused, not because the ceremonies were intrinsically bad, but because the civil magistrate had ordered the ceremonies, being clearly church affairs, without consultation with the pastors. Accordingly, both refused to celebrate the Lord's Supper the following Easter Sunday in their churches because of what they declared was the prevailing immorality of the people in attendance. The breach, which had been growing between the Little Council and the pastors, was now complete. The Little Council summoned the Council of Two Hundred into session two days later and once again these bodies ratified the Bernese ceremonies and then, on April 23, they ordered Farel and Calvin, without a hearing, to leave the city within three days.

On April 25, 1538 the two Reformers left the city, closing Calvin's "first Geneva period." They traveled to Berne where they reported the Geneva government's action, then they pushed on to Zürich where the synod representatives of Basel, Berne, Schaffhausen, St. Gall, and other evangelical territories were meeting on April 28, at which synod they presented their program of ecclesiastical reform. There they urged the frequent observance of the Lord's Supper and the right of church officers to exercise independent use of excommunication when impenitent church members lapsed into sin. The synod approved their position and recommended that the Berne delegates do what they could to seek their restoration to the Genevan church. The Berne delegates obliged, but when they approached Geneva with Calvin and Farel, the Little Council refused to allow Calvin and Farel to enter the city.

Calvin had wanted Geneva to be an orderly, disciplined, Christian city—the city of God on earth—and its church to be self-governing, independent of the control of the civil magistrate. It appeared that his work had been brought permanently to an end there and that he had failed. So Farel and Calvin left Geneva and made their way to Basel to await God's leading.

We leave Calvin now in Basel, a disappointed young Reformer with no job and no source of income. But lest I leave *you* discouraged, may I remind you of the great motto after 1535 of the city of Geneva, *Post Tenebras Lux*—"After darkness, light!" In our next lecture we shall see that light blaze across and light up all of Europe.

CHAPTER THREE

THE MATURE REFORMER OF GENEVA AND HIS ACCOMPLISHMENTS

CALVIN'S MINISTRY AT STRASBOURG

Our second lecture left John Calvin and William Farel in Basel, both having been expelled from Geneva in April 1538 and both without a ministerial call. However, God's call of both was not long in coming: Farel accepted an invitation to pastor in Neuchâtel in July 1538 where he ministered until his death in 1565 (the year following Calvin's death),[1] and Calvin, at the urging of Martin Bucer who had been laboring since 1523 in Strasbourg (at that time in Germany, though now in France), and from whose writings the young Calvin had already learned much, joined Bucer there in September.[2] Bucer's moderating spirit sometimes irritated Calvin, but

---

[1] A public monument honors Farel's memory in Neuchâtel.

[2] Martin Bucer (1491-1551), originally a Dominican monk, became a Lutheran after the Heidelberg Disputation in 1518. He left the cloister and was married in 1522. After his excommunication he took refuge in Strasbourg in 1523 where he assumed a leadership role in the Reformation. There he vigorously sought to adjudicate the hostilities between the Lutherans and Zwinglians on the Lord's Supper. He spent his last years (1548-51) in England, chiefly as Regius Professor of Divinity at Cambridge, where he also preached in St. Mary's Church. After his death and interment his body was later exhumed and was publicly burned during Queen Mary's reign by the Romanist authorities in the Market Square on February 6, 1556.

For more on Bucer and his major work, *On the Reign of Christ*, see H. Eells, *Martin Bucer* (Yale University Press, 1931), and *Melanchthon and Bucer*, edited by Wilhelm Pauck (Library of Christian Classics: Ichthus Edition; Philadelphia: Westminster, 1969), XIX, 155-394.

the more mature Reformer, recognizing Calvin's worth to his Strasbourg Reformation, bore with patience the younger man and assumed the role both of father and prophet to him.

In Strasbourg—one of the greatest of the German Protestant cities and known as the "Antioch of the Reformation"—Calvin organized and pastored the first French-speaking Protestant congregation consisting of about four to six hundred French refugees until 1541 (the "little French Church," he called it), first in the Church of Saint-Nicolas-des-Ondes and then in the Chapel of the Pénitentes de Sainte-Madeleine. There he clarified his views of church organization and established over time a vigorous church discipline independent of the Strasbourg city government such as he had desired for Geneva, and there he developed as well a "Reformed liturgy."

Calvin began to lecture in January 1539 in the Strasbourg *Gymnasium* founded the year before by Johann Sturm, the great Lutheran pedagogue, on the Gospel of John and the Corinthian letters. These lectures attracted wide attention and drew his countrymen from France to Strasbourg to hear him. His fame was rising.

He also published a small psalter for his French congregation with eighteen Psalms (eight of them set to music by Clément Marot and seven by himself) and the Apostles' Creed, all to be sung *a cappella*.

His letters of March 1539 reveal that he attended a conference in Frankfurt, prior to a meeting of an imperial Diet to explore the possibility of reunion with Rome, where he met Philip Melanchthon for the first time and struck up a lasting friendship with him. [3]

---

[3] Philip Melanchthon was born in Bretten, Baden on February 16, 1497. In 1509, the year Calvin was born, he matriculated at the University in Heidelberg at the age of twelve and there earned the Bachelor of Arts at the age of fourteen. When sixteen he earned the

All the while, and more importantly for our purpose, he continued working on his *Institutes*. In August 1539 he published from Strasbourg in Latin the second edition of the *Institutes* that reflected not only his maturing pastoral experience in Strasbourg but also a current of thought

---

Master of Arts at the University of Tübingen. In 1518, at the age of twenty-one, he was called to be professor of Greek at the University of Wittenberg and soon became a close disciple of Martin Luther and an energetic advocate of the Reformation.

His gift for systematic formulation is reflected in his *Loci Communes* (1521), the first systematic statement of Luther's ideas. In 1530 he wrote the *Augsburg Confession* and in 1531 its *Apology*, both documents becoming key statements of Lutheran doctrine. In his 1540 *Variata* of the *Augsburg Confession* he set forth a position on the real presence in the Lord's Supper that was closer to that of Calvin, bringing the accusation from strict Lutherans that Melanchthon was a crypto-Calvinist. After Luther's death in 1546, when Melanchthon argued in the *Leipzig Interim* (1547) that certain Roman Catholic rites and beliefs were adiaphoritic, that is, non-essential to the faith and thus could be accepted, and that man could reject God's grace and the Holy Spirit after grace was given, Matthias Flacius attacked him as a traitor to the Lutheran cause. As a result he spent the last quarter of his life in internecine controversy as many Lutherans, rightly in my opinion, looked upon him increasingly with suspicion. Even Calvin (*Letters*, 2:272) rebuked him for his "large concessions to the Papists" and said he was not surprised that Melanchthon's Lutheran opponents thought he had abandoned them.

He died April 19, 1560 and in spite of the conflicts in his last years with other Lutherans who claimed to be purer Lutherans than he, Melanchthon's contributions to the Lutheran cause are still monumental, so much so that, in my opinion, Lutheran soteriology today in many quarters resembles more that of Melanchthon than that of Luther himself. And because of the large number of cities in Germany through the years that sought his help in bringing reform to their schools and because he assisted in the reform of eight universities and the founding of four others, he came to be known by his thankful students as the "Preceptor of Germany."

different from Lutheranism and more distinctly "Calvinistic"
in content. This much-enlarged edition no longer had only
the six chapters of the first edition that were dependent in
their arrangement on the Lutheran catechism but seventeen
chapters, with new material on man's knowledge of God and
of himself, repentance, justification by faith, the likenesses
and differences of the Old and New Testaments,
predestination, providence, and the life of the Christian man.

In Geneva, meanwhile, much dissension still existed
between the city government and the ministers who had
replaced Farel and Calvin. Seeing in this unrest an opportunity
to reclaim Geneva for Rome, Cardinal Sadoleto, to whom
we referred earlier in connection with our discussion of
Calvin's conversion, wrote the Genevan authorities on March
26, 1539 and appealed to them in fine Latin to return Geneva
to the "ancient faith." The Little Council turned his appeal
over to the authorities in Berne, who in turn, regarding Calvin
as the only man who could write a suitable reply in suitably
fine Latin, asked him to answer it, which he did in six days.
Calvin's "Reply to Cardinal Sadoleto," dated September 1,
1539 was in the hands of the Genevans by September 5,
becoming regarded over time as the most brilliant popular
defense of the Protestant cause that the Reformation ever
produced, for it expressed the thought and feelings of
Protestants everywhere. All that Cardinal Sadoleto's appeal
really managed to accomplish was to bring Calvin all the
more to the forefront of the Reformation[4] and to win him
new respect and support in Geneva.

For more on Melanchthon and his *Loci Communes* see J. W.
Richard, *Philip Melanchthon, the Protestant Preceptor of Germany,
1497-1560* (New York: G. P. Putnam's Sons, 1898) and *Melanchthon
and Bucer*, XIX, 3-152.

[4]Martin Luther informed Martin Bucer in an October 1539 letter
that he had read Calvin's reply "with unusual pleasure," his only
reference to Calvin by name in a letter.

In March 1540 Calvin completed and published his commentary on Romans, the first of many commentaries on virtually all the books of the Old and New Testaments.

That same year, in August, Calvin, finding bachelorhood an inconvenience,[5] married Idelette de Bure, a widowed member of his Strasbourg congregation and mother of two, a boy and girl, in a simple ceremony, with William Farel officiating. Calvin had been instrumental in bringing her Anabaptist husband, now deceased, and his family to the Reformed faith.

Also in June 1540 he attended as an observer the Colloquy that Charles V had evoked at Hagenau to see if the religious conflict between Rome and the Reformers could be healed. He attended also in November of that year as a Strasbourg delegate the Colloquy at Worms where he again met Melanchthon as well as John Eck, Luther's old debate-nemesis, and thereby became acquainted with the leaders and affairs of the German Reformation. Even though he admired Luther very much, Calvin never met Luther himself.

CALVIN'S RETURN TO GENEVA

While he was at the Worms Colloquy an invitation reached him from the Geneva authorities to return to Geneva, a city seemingly bent on destruction, this invitation having been approved on September 21, 1540 by the Little Council and on October 19 by the Council of Two Hundred, who were facing rampant gambling, street-brawls, drunkenness,

---

[5]Calvin had asked Farel and Bucer to find a wife for him, laying out the following specifications: "I am none of those insane lovers who, when once smitten with the fine figure of a woman, embrace also her faults. This only is the beauty which allures me—if she be chaste, obliging, not fastidious, economical, patient, and careful for my health" (Philip Schaff, *History of the Christian Church*, VIII, 414).

adultery even in high places, public indecency, and general anarchy on the part of the Genevan citizenry and who saw Calvin as the only man able to save the city from total riot and for the Reformation.[6] For some months Calvin remained in a quandary between whether he should continue ministering in Strasbourg or return to Geneva, concerning the latter of which choices he wrote to Farel that he would rather endure "a hundred deaths than that cross."

Regensburg Colloquy
In March 1541 he attended the Colloquy at Regensburg (sometimes called Ratisbon) where the discussion, in the presence of the emperor, was conducted between John Eck (whom Calvin characterized as an "impudent babbler and vain sophist"), Johann Gropper, and Julius Pflug on the Roman Catholic side and Philip Melanchthon, Martin Bucer, and Johann Pistorius on the Protestant side. At this Colloquy, presided over by Cardinal Gasparo Contarini who was aided by Albertus Pighius, so-called Catholic "evangelicals" and Protestants came as close as they ever would to crafting a document which would heal the Reformation breach. Even this "healing" document was only accomplished by the two sides producing a compromise statement on original sin and justification by faith (it was weak in its doctrine of imputation). But the Colloquy completely broke down over the doctrine of the Lord's Supper, with the Catholics insisting on their doctrine of transubstantiation and the Protestants, led by Calvin, refusing to tolerate it as being both unscriptural and the idolatrous worship of mere bread as Christ's body,[7]

---

[6]For the political antecedents behind Geneva's invitation to Calvin to resume his ministry there see John C. Olin, "Introduction," in *A Reformation Debate* (Grand Rapids: Baker, 1966), 24-25.

[7]Christians, of course, do not worship the human body or human nature of Jesus *per se* because it is "creaturely" and not divine. They

with Calvin privately faulting Melanchthon and Bucer in a letter to Farel for offering "ambiguous and varnished formulas concerning transubstantiation" in order to "satisfy the opposite party by giving them nothing."

Estimates of the Regensburg Accord on justification have varied: Calvin himself gave it a mixed review. He was delighted that the Catholics had come as far as they did toward the Protestant position on justification (they would not, however, accept the Lutheran *sola* attached to *fide*) but wished for still greater clarity. Luther denounced it as conceding too much to Rome. And Pope Paul III and many Catholics condemned it as conceding too much to Luther. It was a Reformation Age case of each side at the Colloquy, for the sake of healing the breach between them, being willing to allow the other side to see in a carefully crafted document its own view (just as the three unsalutary documents, "Evangelicals and Catholics Together," "The Gift of Salvation," and the "Joint Declaration on the Doctrine of Justification," do in our own time[8]). Rome pronounced Regensburg a failure and cleared the way for the convening of the Council of Trent in 1545. So nothing came from the Colloquy. Calvin's primary concern at the Regensburg Colloquy was to do all he could to heal the division between Lutheranism and Zwinglianism which was proving to be a hindrance to the advance of Protestantism.

Also in 1541 he wrote in French a "Brief Treatise on the Holy Lord's Supper" that laid the foundation of a doctrinal

---

worship the Second Person of the Godhead who became incarnate for us men and for our salvation, whose human body and nature are ever united to the divine Word.

[8]See my *The Reformation Conflict with Rome: Why It Must Continue* (Ross-shire, Scotland: Christian Focus, 2001), 85-98, for my discussion of these contemporary efforts to heal the breach between Protestantism and Roman Catholicism.

Calvinism distinct both from Lutheranism and the doctrine of Zwingli. In it he attempted to bring mutual understanding between the Lutherans and the Zwinglians, about which treatise Martin Luther, impressed by it when he read the 1545 Latin translation because Calvin did not deny the real presence of Christ in the Supper (though he depicted Christ's physical presence as real in a *spiritual* sense), would say: "I might well have relegated the whole matter of this controversy [between Zwingli and me at Marburg twelve years ago] to him from the beginning. I confess for my part if the opposition had done likewise, we might soon have reached an agreement."[9]

That same year Calvin completed his French translation of the 1539 second edition of the *Institutes* from the Latin. Today that French edition is regarded as a French classic and a landmark in the history of French prose, distinguished for its clarity, dignity, and sonorous oratorical sentences.

---

[9]Many Calvinists would be shocked if they knew that Calvin insisted that believers really partake of Jesus' human life (his "flesh" and his "blood") in the sacrament of the Lord's Supper. Disagreeing with his Roman Catholic and Lutheran contemporaries only in the *mode* of that partaking, Calvin believed that the Holy Spirit communicates Christ's flesh and blood to faithful partakers without Christ's needing to leave heaven by lifting them up by faith to Christ in heaven whereby they feed upon his flesh and blood in some ineffable though necessary way. See Keith A. Mathison, *Given for You: Reclaiming Calvin's Doctrine of the Lord's Supper* (Phillipsburg, N. J.: Presbyterian & Reformed, 2001), for a full and sympathetic discussion of Calvin's view. For my discussion of Calvin's view, see my *A New Systematic Theology of the Christian Faith* (Second edition; Nashville, Tennessee: Thomas Nelson, 2002), 961-4, where I note that Charles Hodge thought Calvin's view was "peculiar," Robert Lewis Dabney thought it "strange" and "not only incomprehensible, but impossible," and William Cunningham declared it to be "unsuccessful", "about as unintelligible as Luther's consubstantiation," and "perhaps, the greatest blot in the history of Calvin's labours as a public instructor."

Farel Again

Having made up his mind by this time to leave Strasbourg and to return to Geneva, again because of a "thundering" letter he had received from Farel,[10] Calvin set out for and arrived in Geneva on September 13, 1541—a wiser and more mature pastor than before but still with his *Articles on the Organization of the Church and its Worship* in hand—reflecting his continuing resolve to create in Geneva his vision of the Reformed city: regular preaching and catechetical instruction for children and adults alike, combined with close regulation of the business and moral life of the community. He explained his decision to return to Geneva in a letter to Farel in the following words:

> Had I the choice at my own disposal, nothing would be less agreeable to me than to follow your advice. But when I remember that I am not my own, I offer up my heart, presented as a sacrifice to the Lord.... I submit my will and my affections, subdued and held fast, to the obedience of God.

These words reflect the sentiment in his crest—a hand with a burning heart in it, with the words "I give you all, promptly and sincerely."[11]

---

[10]Perhaps we give too much credit to Farel here and overlook the inner vocational attachment to the Geneva church that Calvin declared was always his in his "Reply to Sadoleto":

> ...though I am for the present relieved of the charge of the Church of Geneva, that circumstance ought not to prevent me from embracing it with paternal affection—God, when he gave it to me in charge, having bound me to be faithful to it for ever.

[11]His "little French church" which he left in Strasbourg eventually moved to England in 1549 but fled from Queen Mary in 1554 to Frankfurt-am-Maim where, because of indiscretions on its pastor's part, it was forced to close in 1562 with some members going to Elizabeth's England and others sharing a church in Frankfurt with English exiles.

Beginning his ministry again in Geneva after his three and a half year "exile" (April 1538 to September 1541), Calvin preached from his pulpit at St. Peter's Church his first Sunday back at the exact place in the biblical text at which he had left off when he was dismissed, and he continued to labor in Geneva without interruption for the next twenty-three years until his death in 1564.

CALVIN'S ACCOMPLISHMENTS AT GENEVA

Calvin's "second Geneva period" (1541-1564) has been generally divided by his biographers and church historians into two distinct periods: his years of struggle (1541-1555), about which we will say something, in which he was often at odds with the Little Council and with his religious enemies, and his years of triumph (1555-1564). Here again, we witness the Genevan motto, *Post Tenebras Lux,* being exhibited. Much could be said about Calvin's ministry during the last nine years of his life when he was finally able to see his concern for a free church in Geneva approved by the Little Council and his energies directed to his writings and to the evangelization of France. But we may summarize his accomplishments during this "Second Geneva Period" by highlighting the following eight categories of activity that he accomplished with the aid and cooperation of a close band of like-minded ministerial colleagues ("the Venerable Company"), all of whom like himself were exiles from France, and the Consistory, a new institution made up of an equal number of ministers and magistrates sitting as elders, that met on a regular basis to supervise the morals and religious life of the community:

1. As a result of the struggles and labors of Calvin and the other Geneva ministers the city's moral and social bearing gradually improved, which influenced many other cities in

Europe that saw Geneva as attempting to live out the principles of religious reform. For these cities, Geneva, emerging as the major powerhouse of religious and cultural reform, became a beacon of hope in an unruly world, so much so that John Knox who studied under Calvin there would later characterize it as "the most perfect school of Christ that ever was on the earth since the days of the Apostles." Because of Geneva's reforming efforts, "the moralizing of social life, the work ethic, the prohibition of begging, aid to the poor—these [became] some distinguishing traits of the Calvinistic city."[12]

2. Calvin finally saw founded in Geneva, not a new state, but a new church—the Protestant church.[13] I will explain what I mean here. Abraham Kuyper observes:

> ...when the question is put, Who had the clearest insight into the reformatory principle, worked it out most fully, and applied it most broadly, history points to the Thinker of Geneva and not to the Hero of Wittenberg. ...in all Lutheran countries [following the principle of Luther and the Lutheran jurists: *Cuius regio eius*

---

[12]Cottret, *Calvin: A Biography*, 165.

[13]The central issue that brought this about, as we have suggested, was Calvin's years-long concern to achieve for the church freedom from the state in ecclesiastical disciplinary matters. And the eventthat brought this matter to a head was a dispute about Philibert Berthelier, a leader of the anti-Calvin party in Geneva. Because of an offense Berthelier had committed, the Consistory had taken action to exclude him from the Lord's Table. But on September 2, 1553, in spite of Calvin's objection and his threat to leave Geneva, the Little Council readmitted him to the Supper. The following day, Sunday, September 3, Berthelier did not approach the Table, having been secretly advised by the Council, fearing that Calvin would indeed leave Geneva, not to do so. Calvin had faced his opposition down, even though it was not until January 24, 1555 that the Council confirmed the Consistory's right to excommunicate.

religio ("Whose the region, his the religion")] the Reformation originated from the princes rather than from the people, and thereby passed under the power of the magistrate, who took his stand in the Church officially as her highest Bishop, and therefore was unable to change either the social or the political life in accordance with its principles.[14]

Calvin's "ideal of a Church, not independent of the State, but autonomous and free to act in its own sphere, came into conflict at every instant with the strict dependency to which the German Churches were subjected by the political power."[15] Consequently, the churches following Calvin's lead in Switzerland, the Netherlands, England, Scotland, and Colonial America—fearing with Calvin the "annexation of the church by the state, a secularization of [its] theology for the benefit of political ideology, [and] the dilution, finally, of the ecclesiastical dignity within the civil hierarchy"[16]— insisted upon freedom from the powers of the magistrate in order to govern themselves, thereby creating the Protestant Church. And these Calvinistic churches

have always struggled…for the liberty, that is to say, for the sovereignty of the Church, within her own sphere, in distinction from the Lutheran theologians. In Christ, they contended, the Church has her own King. Her position in the State is not assigned her by the permission of the government, but *jure divino*. She has her own organization. She possesses her own office-bearers.[17]

---

[14]Abraham Kuyper, *Lectures on Calvinism* (Grand Rapids: Eerdmans, 1931), 22-3.

[15]Francois Wendel, *Calvin*, translated by Philip Mairet (London: Collins, 1963), 64-5.

[16]Cottret, *Calvin: A Biography*, 164.

[17]The free church of Geneva, as did Bucer's Strasbourg church, had four office holders: pastors to preach and to distribute the sacraments, doctors to teach, elders to "amicably admonish those they see are at fault and leading a disorderly life," and deacons to watch over the poor and the sick.

And in a similar way she has her own gifts to distinguish truth from the lie. It is therefore her privilege, and not that of the State, to determine her own characteristics as the true Church, and to proclaim her own confession as the confession of the truth.[18]

With all this Benjamin B. Warfield concurs. Accordingly, he concludes:

...every Church in Protestant Christendom which enjoys today any liberty whatever, in performing its functions as a Church of Jesus Christ, owes it all to John Calvin. It was he who first asserted this liberty in his early manhood...; it was he who first gained it in a lifelong struggle against a determined opposition; it was he who taught his followers to value it above life itself, and to secure it to their successors with the outpouring of their blood. And thus Calvin's great figure rises before us as not only in a true sense the creator of the Protestant Church, but the author of all the freedom it exercises in its spiritual sphere.[19]

3. As we mentioned in our second lecture, Calvin had continued over the years to supervise improvements in the accuracy of translation and the language of Olivétan's French translation of the Bible. His labors, with the assistance of Theodore Beza and Louis Budé, finally produced the French "Geneva Bible," published by Robert Estienne in Geneva in 1553, that dominated French-speaking Protestantism for two centuries.

4. Around 1555 the Venerable Company of Pastors in Geneva, together with the Consistory, in response to requests for help from Calvinist congregations in France,

---

[18]Kuyper, *Lectures*, 105-6.

[19]Benjamin B. Warfield, "John Calvin: The Man and His Work," *The Works of Benjamin B. Warfield*, V, 19. See Appendix B where I note a significant effect of Calvin's view of the church free from state control and the state free from church control. I have placed this material in an appendix rather than at this place in the lecture because I did not include it in this lecture when it was originally given.

secretly began to infiltrate France with well-trained pastors[20] so that by 1562[21] the number of consistories (sessions of elders) in France numbered 1,785 and as many as 2,150 Huguenot churches existed with a total membership well in excess of two million out of a national French population of twenty million. These Genevan church leaders also commissioned missionaries to go as far as Brazil to spread the gospel.

5. Evidencing his "Christian humanism," Calvin also founded the famous Geneva Academy on June 5, 1559—destined to

---

[20]Between 1555 and 1562 the Venerable Company, according to its *Register*, commissioned 97 missionaries to minister in France.

[21]The reason I mention the year 1562 is that this was the year the Wars of Religion began in France, which wars continued until the Edict of Nantes in 1598. They included the treacherous St. Bartholomew's Day Massacres in 1572 of some 20,000 Huguenots, which horrible crime was approved and sanctioned by the papacy. Pope Gregory XIII rejoiced when the news of these murders reached him and he commissioned a mural to be painted, had salutes fired from the fortress St. Angelo, ordered a special *Te Deum*, and had a commemorative seal struck to honor the occasion, regarding it a pious deed that a Catholic king would slaughter his subjects simply because they were Protestants! The Edict of Nantes brought only temporary cessation of the Huguenot persecution, however, and by 1685, when Louis XIV revoked the Edict of Nantes, most of the Huguenots had already fled France anyway, to that nation's great and lasting loss. This is one reason that Calvin's reputation is so ambiguous in his own country today: the French people simply do not know much about him as a person, about his thought, or about his followers. In sum, Calvinism became a lost cause in France, and today France is around 92 percent atheistic or agnostic, the least religious nation in Europe. But by that time Calvinism had made gains elsewhere; indeed, it had become an international religious movement.

For the story of these French Protestants see Janet Glenn Gray, *The French Huguenots: Anatomy of Courage* (Grand Rapids: Baker, 1981).

become the first Protestant "university" in the world and the central educational institution of the Reformed church whose international influence over time far surpassed even the University of Wittenberg during Luther's lifetime. Calvin became its leading professor of theology, to which in time more than a thousand students from all parts of Europe sat daily to attend the lectures of Calvin and Beza, the Academy's first rector, and from which went forth missionaries throughout Europe and to the New World.

The Influence of the Students of the Academy
Something should be said here about the influence of these students of the Geneva Academy.[22] Among them were Guido de Bray who would write the *Belgic Confession* in 1561 and Caspar Olevianus who together with Zacharias Ursinus would write the famous *Heidelberg Catechism* in 1563. Also many Protestants had fled Britain for Geneva under the persecution of Mary Tudor ("Bloody Mary"), among them Miles Coverdale, John Foxe (author of *Foxe's Book of Martyrs*), and John Knox who later brought church and cultural reform to all of Scotland and thus became the founder not only of Scottish and English Puritanism but also of American Puritanism through Scottish migration to the New World.[23] Calvin's students also carried the Calvinistic

---

[22]One of the better books in this connection is *John Calvin: His Influence in the Western World*, edited by W. Stanford Reid (Grand Rapids: Zondervan, 1982). Each of its sixteen chapters highlights an influence of Calvin on some area in the West including France, the Netherlands, Germany, Hungary, England, Scotland, New England, Canada, Australasia, and South Africa. A second book treating the influence of Calvin on the five governments of Geneva, France, Scotland, England, and Colonial America is Douglas F. Kelly's *The Emergence of Liberty in the Modern World* (Phillipsburg, N. J.: Presbyterian and Reformed, 1992).

[23]So D. Martyn Lloyd-Jones, *The Puritans: Their Origins and Successors* (Edinburgh: Banner of Truth, 1987), 278. John Knox (c.

world-view they learned in Geneva back to their homes in France, Germany, Poland, Bohemia, Hungary, Holland, Belgium, England, Wales, and Scotland, and eventually to the New World.

Calvin's teaching on religious freedom, in particular, laid the foundation for Reformed Presbyterianism, and his views spread from the Geneva Academy throughout Europe, and

---

1514-72) was educated at St. Andrews University in Scotland. After his conversion to Protestantism he came under the influence of George Wishart (later burned by Cardinal Beaton) from whom he learned his basic theology, an amalgam of Lutheran and Reformed ideas. After spending nineteen months as a galley slave on a French ship for supporting a group of Protestant rebels in the castle at St. Andrews, he returned to England and there became a powerful preacher (1549-53), but when the Catholic Mary Tudor ("Bloody Mary"), Henry VIII's older daughter, became queen in 1553, he fled to Frankfurt (1553-55) and Geneva (1555-59) where he came under Calvin's influence. In Geneva he also wrote a series of tracts advocating political disobedience to idolatrous (that is, Roman Catholic) rulers, the best known of these being his *First Blast of the Trumpet Against the Monstrous Regiment and Empire of Woman* (1558) in which he denied the right to women to rule. A group of Protestant lords invited him to return to Catholic Scotland in 1559, and his preaching at St. Giles Church in Edinburgh and his uncompromising leadership became major factors in the success of the Scottish Reformation. Three or more times he confronted Mary (Stuart), Queen of Scots, and condemned her Catholic idolatry. After she abdicated the throne in 1567 for moral indiscretions Knox preached at the coronation of her infant son, James VI. He helped draft the *Scots Confession of Faith* (1560) and the *First Book of Discipline* for the Church of Scotland.

His literary output fills six volumes, his only academic theological work being his *Treatise on Predestination* (1559) and his greatest work being his *History of the Reformation of Religion within the Realm of Scotland*.

I highly recommend W. Stanford Reid's *Trumpeter of God: A Biography of John Knox* (New York: Charles Scribner's Sons, 1974) to any reader who wants to know more about this Scottish Reformer.

from these European countries, especially from the British Isles, Presbyterianism spread to the New World where it became very influential in the original American colonies through the Geneva Bible and in both the "Great Awakening" through the efforts of such men as Gilbert Tenant in the North and Samuel Davies in the South and the American Revolution itself through the preaching of such men as John Witherspoon (the only minister to sign the Declaration of Independence), George Duffield and James Caldwell. Interestingly, when news of the American Revolution reached England, Horace Walpole rose from his seat in the British House of Commons and wryly commented: "There is no crying about the matter. Cousin America has run off with a Presbyterian parson, and that is the end of it."[24]

It is also an interesting though little known fact that at the time of the American Revolutionary War an estimated three million people lived in the colonies, of which number nine hundred thousand were of Scotch or Scotch-Irish (or "Ulster Scots") descent, six hundred thousand were Puritan English, while four hundred thousand were of Dutch, German Reformed, and Huguenot descent. This means that roughly two-thirds of America's Revolutionary forebears had been trained in the religious and political thought of Calvin, with more than one-half of all the officers and soldiers of the American army during the Revolution being Presbyterians.

The "Geneva Bible"

Other English Protestants who came to Geneva as a result of Mary's persecution were William Whittington and Anthony Gilby who, under the protection of the Genevan

---

[24]Douglas F. Kelly in his *The Emergence of Liberty in the Modern World*, 131, observes: "The gibe of some in the British Parliament that the America Revolution was a 'Presbyterian Rebellion' did not miss the mark."

civil authorities and with Calvin's encouragement and support, along with other English scholars there, translated into English from the original Hebrew and Greek what has come to be known as the "Geneva Bible." It was instantly popular in England, becoming the most widely read and influential English Bible of the sixteenth and seventeenth centuries—more popular even than the King James Version—over two-hundred printings of it appearing between 1560, when it was first published in Geneva, and 1644, the last year it was printed. It was the Geneva Bible, *not* the King James Version, that the Pilgrims brought with them to America when they sailed on the *Mayflower* in 1620 to the New World and it was the Geneva Bible that was the generally accepted Bible among the colonial Puritans.

What made the Geneva Bible so popular? The key feature of the Geneva Bible that distinguished it from all the other Bibles of its time and that led to its popularity were the extensive marginal notes that explained the Scriptures to the common people. These notes, approximately three hundred thousand words in length, occupied one-third of the total content of the Geneva Bible. They were written by Calvin, Knox, Coverdale, Whittington, Gilby, William Keithe, Thomas Sampson, Thomas Wood and others. Another helpful feature, on the advice of Calvin, was the Geneva Bible's division of chapters into numbered verses, the first Bible to do so.

The marginal notes, which made it so popular, became also the reason for its demise. These strongly Protestant notes, particularly those that allowed for disobedience to kings (such as the note on Exod. 1:19) infuriated King James I of England who, considering the notes "seditious," made ownership of the Geneva Bible a felony. Moreover, James I authorized the production of a new Bible which drew largely for its translation from the Geneva Bible minus, of course, its marginal notes. Thus this much-loved version of the Bible, the King James Version of 1611, was in fact first published primarily to eliminate the influence of the notes of the Geneva Bible on the English populace. Nevertheless, here we see yet again, through the influence of the Geneva Bible on the English Puritans who came to America, how we Americans, whether we realize it or not, are beneficiaries of Calvin's thought and ministry.

These are a few of the reasons that have led historians such as Leopold von Ranke and J. H. Merle D'Aubigne to declare, rightly or wrongly, that through his followers John Calvin was "the virtual founder of America." John Adams, our second president, wrote: "Let not Geneva be forgotten or despised. Religious liberty owes [that city] most respect." And American historian George Bancroft stated: "He that will not honor the memory and respect the influence of Calvin knows but little of the origin of American liberty."

6. Calvin preached some four thousand sermons during this period, some two thousand of which are available to the modern reader.[25] Obviously, this means that Calvin preached often as his health permitted: on weekdays, every other week, he preached from the Old Testament at 6 a.m. (7 a.m. in the winter), on Sunday mornings from the New Testament, and on Sunday afternoons from the Psalms, averaging slightly over one hundred and seventy sermons a year.

---

[25]We have these sermons because the Venerable Company of Pastors in Geneva hired a Frenchman, Denis Raguenier, who had developed a system of shorthand that enabled him to write down Calvin's sermons of about six thousand words each with a quill pen and ink, in an unheated church winter and summer, for the better part of an hour at a time. Calvin himself did not revise them or have anything to do with them after he had preached them. Raguenier recorded the sermons, transcribed them, and bound them in sets. As a result, we have, for example, 89 sermons on Acts between 1549 and 1554, a shorter series on some of the Pauline letters between 1554 and 1558,

7. Calvin's literary output during this period is truly amazing. He wrote commentaries on most of the books of the Bible in both Latin and French[26] that are still being used today by pastors and biblical scholars, dedicating them to kings and queens, princes and dukes.[27] He wrote three catechisms

and 65 sermons on the Harmony of the Gospels between 1559 and 1564. During this same time, on weekday mornings he preached series of sermons on Jeremiah and Lamentations up to 1550, on the Minor Prophets and Daniel from 1550 to 1552, 174 sermons on Ezekiel from 1552 to 1554, 159 sermons on Job from 1554 to 1555, 200 sermons on Deuteronomy from 1555 to 1556, 342 sermons on Isaiah from 1556 to 1559, 123 sermons on Genesis from 1559 to 1561, a short series on Judges in 1561, 107 sermons on 1 Samuel and 87 sermons on 2 Samuel from 1561 to 1563, and a series on 1 Kings in 1563 and 1564.

[26]For more information on Calvin's commentaries see *Calvin: Commentaries*, edited by Joseph Haroutunian (Library of Christian Classics; Philadelphia: Westminster, 1958), Volume XXIII.

[27]Calvin's commentary dedications illustrate his wide European interests, as the following data will disclose: he originally dedicated his 1554 commentary on Genesis to the three sons of Johann Frederick, Elector of Saxony, but the princes, at the suggestion of Lutheran theologians, rejected the dedication because Calvin deviated from the Lutheran doctrine of the Lord's Supper. He dedicated the 1563 edition, which appeared along with Exodus through Deuteronomy, to Henry of Bourbon (later King Henry IV of France) who was ten years old at the time.

He dedicated the 1551 edition of his commentary on Isaiah to Edward VI, King of England, and the 1559 second edition to Queen Elizabeth of England, Edward's sister, while retaining the original dedication to Edward. Elizabeth rejected the dedication because she thought Calvin was behind John Knox's *First Blast of the Trumpet Against the Monstrous Regiment and Empire of Women* that was written from Geneva. Calvin's attempt to heal the breach with Elizabeth proved futile, even though he did not approve of Knox's treatise and had not known anything about it prior to its publication.

He dedicated his 1563 commentary on Jeremiah and Lamentations to Duke Frederick III, Lord Palatine of the Rhine, Elector of the

(1537, 1542, 1545), all for the city of Geneva, several confessions of faith (the Zürich Consensus of 1549 and 1551, the Geneva Consensus of 1552, and the French Confession of 1559 and 1562), and many theological

---

Roman Empire, his 1561 commentary on Daniel to the "pious worshipers of God who desire the Kingdom of Christ to be rightly constituted in France," and his 1559 commentary on the Minor Prophets to Gustavus Vasa, King of the Goths and Vandals (Sweden), who had introduced the Lutheran Reformation there (the book was not met with appreciation).

He dedicated his 1555 Harmony of Matthew, Mark, and Luke to the Council of Frankfurt; his 1553 commentary on John to the Syndics and Council of Geneva; his 1552 commentary on Acts, vol. 1, to Christian III, King of Denmark, and his 1554 commentary on Acts, vol. 2, to Crown Prince Frederick of Denmark (the 1560 second edition of Acts to Nicolas Radziwill, Duke in Olika, Lord Chancellor of the Dukedom of Lithuania); his 1540 commentary (his first) on Romans to Simon Grynaeus, professor of Latin and Greek at Heidelberg; his 1546 first edition of 1 Corinthians to James of Burgundy, Lord of Falais and Breda, with whom later he had a "falling out" over James's endorsement of Jérome-Hermès Bolsec's doctrine of election, which led to his dedicating his 1556 second edition of 1 Corinthians to Galeazzo Caraccioli di Vico, a distinguished Italian who had settled in Geneva; his 1547 commentary on 2 Corinthians to Melchior Wolmar, his first Greek teacher; his 1548 commentaries on Galatians, Ephesians, Philippians, Colossians to Christopher, Duke of Würtemberg, who had introduced Lutheran thought in Mont-béliard; his 1550 commentary on 1 Thessalonians to Mathurin Cordier, his childhood Latin instructor; his 1550 commentary on 2 Thessalonians to Benedict Textor, his family physician; his 1548 commentary on 1 and 2 Timothy to Edward Seymour, Duke of Somerset and Lord Protector of England as the guardian of the minor King Edward VI; his 1549 commentary on Titus to William Farel and Peter Viret; his 1549 commentary on Hebrews to Sigismund August II, King of Poland and Duke of Lithuania, Russia, Prussia, and Lord of Muscovy; and his 1550 commentary on the Catholic Epistles to Edward VI, King of England (in the dedication Calvin writes extensively about the Council of Trent).

Calvin's other commentaries carry no dedication from his hand.

treatises[28] against the Roman Catholic Church,[29] the Anabaptists and the Libertines,[30] and the Anti-Trinitarians (Servetus, 1554; Valentinus Gentilis, 1561; Socinians, 1561, 1563), as well as two major defenses of the doctrine of predestination against Bolsec and Castellio (1554 and 1557), two major defenses of the doctrine of the Lord's Supper against the hard-line Lutheran Joachim Westphal (1555 and 1556), a smaller essay on the same subject against Tilemann Heshusius (1561), another Lutheran, and a minor treatise against astrology (1549).

Let us sample one of his better known treatises against Rome, "An Admonition, Showing the Advantages that Christendom Might Derive from an Inventory of Relics,"[31] written in 1543, in which, in order to accomplish his desired effect, he endlessly and monotonously enumerates, out of the four thousand dioceses, thirty thousand abbacies, forty thousand monasteries, and the multitude of parishes and chapels that existed then throughout Europe, the relics of which he was aware in only six or so German cities, three or so cities in Spain, fifteen in Italy, and between thirty and forty in France that were on display for the people's veneration.

---

[28]For more information on Calvin's theological treatises see *Calvin: Theological Treatises*, edited by J. K. S. Reid (Library of Christian Classics; Philadelphia: Westminster, 1954), Volume XXII.

[29]See particularly here Calvin's *The Bondage and Liberation of the Will: A Defence of the Orthodox Doctrine of Human Choice against Pighius*, edited by A. N. S. Lane and translated by G. I. Davies (Grand Rapids: Baker, 1996).

[30]See John Calvin, *Treatises Against the Anabaptists and Against the Libertines*, edited and translated by Benjamin Wirt Farley (Grand Rapids: Baker, 1982).

[31]This treatise may be found in *Selected Works of John Calvin: Tracts and Letters*, edited and translated by Henry Beveridge (Reprint; Grand Rapids: Baker, 1983), 1, 289-341.

Calvin begins his itemization of relics: With respect to Christ these relics included his teeth, his hair, his sandals, and his blood, not to mention the manger in which he was laid at birth, the clothes in which he was wrapped as a babe, the cradle in which his mother later laid him, the altar on which he was circumcised, and his foreskin—displayed at three different sites simultaneously (!); a picture of him when he was twelve years old, a pillar against which he leaned while disputing in the Temple, the water pots employed in his first miracle including some of the wine he created on that occasion, five pieces of the bread he created when he fed the five thousand, and the earth on which he stood when he raised Lazarus from the dead; the branch he purportedly carried when he rode into Jerusalem, the tail of the ass on which he rode, the table of the last Passover, some of the bread he broke on that occasion, the knife which was used to cut up the Paschal Lamb, two cups, one in a church near Lyons and one in an Augustinian monastery, both purported to have contained the sacrament of his blood, three dishes—at Rome, at Genoa, and at Arles—all purported to have been the dish in which the Paschal Lamb was placed, the linen towel—one at Rome and another at Acqs, the latter with the mark of Judas' foot on it—with which Jesus wiped the disciples' feet; the money which Judas received to betray Jesus, and the steps of Pilate's judgment seat (the steps that Luther climbed); his cross the fragments of which if gathered together, Calvin estimated, would require more than three hundred men to carry; the tablet that Pilate ordered affixed over the cross—but displayed both at Rome and at Toulouse simultaneously; fourteen nails purported to be the nails driven into his hands and feet, the soldier's spear—displayed at Rome, also at Paris, yet again at Saintonge, and still a fourth at Selve; the crown of thorns, a third part of which is at Paris, three thorns of which are at Rome, one at Vincennes, five at Bourges, three at Besançon, and three at Königsberg, an unknown number in Spain, and twelve in almost as many cities in France; the robe in which Pilate clothed Jesus located at least four different sites; the reed placed in his hand as a mock scepter, the dice that were used to gamble for his robe, and the sponge containing vinegar mixed with gall that was offered to him at the cross; the napkin that was wrapped about his head in burial—but on display in eight different cities simultaneously, and a piece of the broiled fish Peter offered him after his resurrection, not to mention the numerous claims of possessing his footprints as well as crucifixes that grew beards, that spoke, and that shed tears.

With regard to Mary, Calvin continued, two churches claimed to possess the body of Anne, her mother, while three churches claimed to possess one of Anne's hands. The churches displayed Mary's hair, her combs, pieces of her wardrobe, four pictures of her purported to have been painted by Luke, a very valuable wedding ring purported to have been Mary's, and even vials of her milk, with so many towns, so many monasteries, so many nunneries laying claim here that, as Calvin writes, "had she continued to nurse during her whole lifetime, she scarcely could have furnished the quantity which is exhibited."

Six different churches, Calvin notes, claimed to possess the finger John the Baptist used when he pointed his disciples to Jesus, while others claimed to possess John's sandals, his girdle, the altar on which he purportedly prayed in the desert, and the sword that was used to cut off his head. Two churches claimed to have the bodies of the Magi, three churches claimed to have Lazarus' body, and two churches claimed to have Mary Magdalene's body.

With regard to the apostles, Calvin continued, the church at Lyons claimed to possess the twelve combs they used. Half of Peter's body and Paul's body was said to be at St. Peter's, half at St. Paul's, while the heads of both were purportedly located in a third church. This did not stop other churches from claiming to have Peter's cheekbone, many bones belonging to both, and one claimed to have Paul's shoulder. Rome claimed to have the sword Peter used to cut off Malchus' ear, the "throne" on which he sat, and the robe in which he was attired when he officiated at the altar at which he said Mass, the chain with which he was bound, and the pillar on which he was beheaded.

Regarding the rest of the apostles, Calvin continued, the church at Toulouse claimed to have six of their bodies, namely, those of James the greater, James the Less, Andrew, Philip, Simeon, and Jude. But Andrew had another body at Melfi, Philip and James the Less each had another body at the Church of the Holy Apostles, and Simeon and Jude had second bodies at St. Peter's. Bartholomew's body was exposed both at Naples and at Rome simultaneously. Three different churches claimed to have the body of Matthias, with a fourth claiming to possess his head and his arm. Most were purported to have body parts on display throughout the realms.

Stephen's entire body, Calvin continues, is purportedly in the church that bears his name in Rome, but his head is also at Arles and more than two hundred of his bones are in other places.[32] They also display the stones that were used to kill him.

Rome even boasted of possessing the relics of an angel— Michael's dagger and shield.

Foregoing the mention of myriad other relics and duplications of bodies and body parts of which he knew, "lest I get entangled in a forest out of which I should never be

---

[32]It did not seem to bother the fathers of Trent that the same object was venerated in different places. Jean Ferrand, the seventeenth-century Jesuit, even contended that such objects as the wood of the cross and the crown of thorns were so necessary for devotion to God that God arranged their miraculous replication.

able to escape," Calvin concludes this treatise by calling upon Christians to abolish the corrupt and heathen practice of the veneration of relics.

We will return now to his literary output. Calvin also wrote forty-two hundred and seventy-one letters of which we are aware (filling ten and a half volumes)—some of these letters virtually treatises in length, some practically theological tractates—written to kings, other heads of state, to statesmen and men of affairs, to Catholic and Reformation leaders in other lands, to pastors, to friends, and to heretics. Among them are his one hundred and sixty-three letters to Farel and his two hundred and four letters to Peter Viret,[33] his two dearest friends who had labored with him in Geneva. His faithful secretary, Charles de Jonvillers, who made many long and expensive journeys later to recover them from their recipients collected many of his letters over a twenty-year period after his death.[34]

---

[33]Peter Viret (1511-1571), the chief Reformer at Lausanne, was born in Orbe, Switzerland and was educated in Paris for the priesthood. He renounced Romanism for Protestantism before he was ordained to the priesthood and returned to Switzerland where under Farel's inducement he preached with great success for a time at his birth-city. He labored also with Farel in Geneva for a time. He was, along with Farel, a chief advocate for the Protestant cause at the Lausanne Disputation in 1536. As a result Viret was appointed to a preaching position in Lausanne where he labored for twenty-two years, but when his efforts to introduce a strict discipline met with much opposition there, just as did Calvin at Geneva and Farel at Neuchâtel, he was deposed in 1559. He then went to Geneva where he was appointed preacher of the city. However, in 1566 he accepted a teaching position at an academy at Orthez where, as the last of the triumvirate (Farel, Calvin, Viret) of the founders of the Reformed Church in Geneva, he labored until his death.

[34]See Henry F. Henderson, *Calvin in His Letters* (Eugene, Oregon: Wipf and Stock, 1996).

8. Most important, perhaps, he saw the *Institutes of the Christian Religion*, his *opus magnum*, through the publication of its 1543 and 1550 Latin editions—both twenty-one chapters with new material on vows and monasticism—and finally he saw published the *last and definitive* 1559 Latin edition of the *Institutes* that is divided into the four books[35] comprising the eighty chapters that we know and study today.[36] The structure of the 1559 edition is generally arranged according to the topics of the Apostles Creed:

Book One: "The Knowledge of God the Creator" (God)
Book Two: "The Knowledge of God the Redeemer in Christ"(Christ)
Book Three: "The Way In Which We Receive the Grace of Christ" (Holy Spirit)
Book Four: "The External Means or Aids By Which God Invites Us Into the Society of Christ and Holds Us Therein" (Church and Sacrament).

And about the arrangement of the material in the final 1559 *Institutes* Calvin writes in his note: "John Calvin to the Reader, 1559": "I was never satisfied until the work had been arranged in the order now set forth. Now I trust I have provided something that all of you will approve."

General Characteristics of the *Institutes*
It is appropriate to mention here the following five general characteristics of this last edition:

---

[35]The four books become increasingly longer in the Battles translation, Book One being 202 pages long, Book Two 293 pages long, Book Three 470 pages long, and Book Four 512 pages long.

[36]Calvin's *Institutes* has been translated into Spanish (1540), Italian (1557), Dutch (1560), French (partially by Calvin himself in 1560), German (1572), Czech (1617), Hungarian (1624), Japanese (1934), Korean, and portions in Chinese. As a result his influence has been and is today truly worldwide.

a. Above everything else the *Institutes* strives to be biblical.
I do not place this first because I *hope* that it is biblical. As
a Christian humanist governed by the *ad fontes* ("back to
the sources") principle, Calvin self-consciously strove to
be biblical in everything he wrote. He was a "wholesale
plagiarist" of Scripture. The forty pages of Scripture
references—2474 Old Testament citations and 4330 New
Testament citations, to be precise—in the "Scripture Index"
of *The Library of Christian Classics* edition (2.1553-92)
attest to this characteristic of the *Institutes*.

As a master exegete of Scripture, his approach to the
exposition of Scripture established sound canons of
interpretation and thus provided direction for all future
exegetical study. And because of his concern always to take
into account the unity and harmony of Scripture teaching
(the "analogy of Scripture" principle) Calvin also became a
master of theological substance, order and proportion, and
in his *Institutes* he presented an orderly arrangement of the
system of truth set forth in the Word of God. However, he
was willing to leave some elements unaddressed if he thought
the Bible had fallen silent on a matter (see *Institutes*,
3.6.1).[37] And while Calvin was willing to deal with a text

---

[37]To illustrate Calvin's submissive spirit to Holy Scripture, expressed
in many places, one may cite what he says when dealing with God's
divine and triune nature:

Here, indeed, if anywhere in the secret mysteries of Scripture, we
ought to play the philosopher soberly and with great moderation;
let us use great caution that neither our thoughts nor our speech go
beyond the limits to which the Word of God extends itself...we
shall be "leaving it to him" if we conceive him to be as he reveals
himself to us, without inquiring about him elsewhere than from his
Word...let us not take it into our heads either to seek out God
anywhere else than in his Sacred Word, or to think anything about
him that is not prompted by his Word, or speak anything that is not
taken from that Word (1.13.21).

critically, as one can readily see from his commentaries, it is evident that where the Bible took him, there he went; where its declarations ceased, there he stopped too, but always giving the benefit of the doubt to Scripture as God's inspired and therefore inerrant Word.[38]

b. Also important, the *Institutes*, theologically considered, is Reformed—which statement is a truism if ever there were one! Its "Calvinistic" theology transcends what is often represented to be the "Calvinism" of the so-called TULIP acronym,[39] though it certainly includes the theology of the TULIP,[40] to entail a holistic Calvinistic world-and-life-view

---

[38]Scholars debate whether Calvin viewed the Bible as inerrant. I say he did. His classic statements in this regard are found in *Institutes*, 4.8.6, 8, 9, his dedicatory letter to his commentary on Romans, and in his commentary on 2 Timothy 3:16. In the just-mentioned dedicatory letter Calvin states:

> Such veneration we ought indeed to entertain for the Word of God, that we ought not to pervert it in the least degree by varying expositions; for its majesty is diminished, I know not how much, especially when not expounded with great discretion and with great sobriety. And if it be deemed a great wickedness to contaminate any thing that is dedicated to God, he surely cannot be endured, who, with impure, or even with unprepared hands, will handle that very thing, which of all things is the most sacred on earth. It is therefore an audacity, closely allied to sacrilege, rashly to turn Scripture in any way we please, and to indulge our fancies as in sport, which has been done by many in former times.

[39]T—the doctrine of total depravity; U—the doctrine of unconditional election; L—the doctrine of limited (that is, particular) atonement; I—the doctrine of irresistible grace; P—the doctrine of the perseverance of the saints.

[40]It is particularly the L—limited or particular atonement—of the TULIP that some Calvin scholars urge was foreign to Calvin's theology. But see my *A New Systematic Theology of the Christian Faith* (Second edition; Nashville, Tennessee: Thomas Nelson, 2002),

(*Weltanschauung*). In the Calvinistic theology of the *Institutes*, as Robert D. Knudsen notes, (1) there is no dichotomy between Christianity and culture; (2) all of life, including human culture, is theonomous, that is, it derives its meaning in its being subject to God and to his law; and (3) the most holy, wise, and powerful providence of the sovereign God embraces the entire course of history.[41]

Battles sees throughout the *Institutes* a Reformed "antithetical structuring," that is, at the same time Calvin sets forth a doctrine, he opposes it against Rome on the one hand and the Radical (Anabaptist[42]) Reformers on the other.[43]

Scholars continue to debate two issues that are related to one another: first, what is the unifying theological theme of the *Institutes*, and second, was Calvin a "covenant theologian?"

***The unifying theme of the* Institutes**. Older Calvin scholars suggested such themes as the sovereignty of God and his

---

672, fn 3, where I show that Calvin did indeed subscribe to the doctrine of particular atonement.

[41]Robert D. Knudsen, "Calvinism as a Cultural Force," *John Calvin: His Influence in the Western World*, 14.

[42]The "Anabaptists" rejected infant baptism and believed in "rebaptism" for those who had been baptized as infants. Also, they were far more concerned with issues of sanctification than the doctrine of justification by faith alone. They also called for radical separation from the world and urged pacifism. In all these respects the leaders of the Magisterial Reformation found it necessary to oppose them.

Readers desiring more information on the Anabaptists will find helpful here *Spiritual and Anabaptist Writers*, edited by George Huntston Williams and Angel M. Mergal (Library of Christian Classics; Philadelphia: Westminster, 1957), Volume XXV; George H. Williams, *The Radical Reformation* (Philadelphia: Westminster, 1962); and William R. Estep, *The Anabaptist Story* (Grand Rapids: Eerdmans, 1975). For a concise and sympathetic treatment of Anabaptist theology see Robert Friedmann, *The Theology of Anabaptism: An Interpretation* (Scottdale, Pennsylvania: Herald, 1973).

[43]Ford Lewis Battles, *Analysis of the Institutes* (Phillipsburg, N.J.: Presbyterian and Reformed, 2001), 19-23.

decrees, Christ, union with Christ, election, and so on, as the unifying theme. But Calvin does not use these to structure his theology. Election, for example, is not taken up until Book III, after "Faith." More recent scholars have urged that there is *no central theme*. Battles declares that

> for man, it is a handbook of piety. But what is it toward God? The *Institutes of the Christian Religion* is a bold effort truly to own God as King of His people (3.20.43). That God may rule among the nations—is this not the central theme of Calvin's theology? God is King.[44]

While this is true enough, for myself, I would say, first, with McNeill that in his *Institutes* Calvin "emphasizes the *centrality* of revelation in both the structure and the content of [his] theology,"[45] but second, with Warfield, that the *theological* reason for this emphasis on the centrality of revelation is that, more fundamentally, the foundation of the entirety of Calvin's thinking was *the vision of God and his majesty as revealed in Jesus Christ.*[46] In short, he was concerned to let the God who had revealed himself in the Second Person of the Godhead *be* for mankind the all-glorious God that he is.

Was Calvin a "covenant theologian?" Some scholars, such as Perry Miller[47] and Charles C. Ryrie,[48] have argued that

---

[44]Battles, *Analysis*, 18.

[45]John T. McNeill (ed.), *Calvin: Institutes of the Christian Religion*, 35, fn. 1.

[46]Benjamin B. Warfield, "The Theology of Calvin," *Calvin and Augustine* (Philadelphia, Pennsylvania: Presbyterian and Reformed, 1956), 491.

[47]Perry Miller, *The New England Mind* (New York: Macmillan, 1939), 366-7.

[48]Charles C. Ryrie, *Dispensationalism Today* (Chicago: Moody, 1965), 179-80.

Calvin had virtually no theology of the covenant and that in this respect a discontinuity exists between Calvin and the later "federal" theologians of the seventeenth century such as Johannes Cocceius (1603-1669) of the Netherlands. Other scholars, such as Geerhardus Vos and Lyle D. Bierma, contend that the covenant idea is indeed discernible in Calvin's theology, Vos arguing that, while Calvin did not use the covenant idea as the organizing principle of his theology, he did employ it in specific discussions,[49] and Bierma arguing that the level of difference between Calvin and the later Reformed thinkers is that of teacher and student, his students developing the idea more fully than did their teacher and making it integral to Reformed theology.[50]

While I think we must admit that there is a difference between Calvin and his theological successors, this admission should not be construed to mean either that Calvin was ignorant of the covenant concept or that a discontinuity exists between him and later Reformed thinkers. Their difference is one only of degree and not one of kind. Because he developed his *Institutes* generally along Trinitarian lines, admittedly the covenant concept is not the architectonic or governing principle of the *Institutes*. But Calvin does employ the unity of the covenant and the oneness of the people of God in all ages when the topic under discussion called for it (see *Institutes*, 2.10.2). Peter Lillback notes that in the 1559 edition of the *Institutes* he used the Latin *pactum* and related cognates thirty-five times, *foedus* and its cognates one hundred and fifty-four times, and

---

[49]Geerhardus Vos, "The Doctrine of the Covenant in Reformed Theology," in *Redemptive History and Biblical Interpretation: The Shorter Writings of Geerhardus Vos*, edited by Richard B. Gaffin Jr. (Phillipsburg, N. J., Presbyterian and Reformed, 1980), 236.

[50]Lyle D. Bierma, *German Calvinism in the Confessional Age: The Covenant Theology of Caspar Olevianus* (Grand Rapids: Baker, 1996), 44-5, 148-51.

testamentum eighty-four times, for a total of two-hundred and seventy-three times (see, for example, *Institutes*, 2.9-11).[51] While the number of times an author uses words may mean little regarding the emphasis he gives to a concept, these statistics do indicate that Calvin was not ignorant of the biblical concept of covenant. And as a student of law Calvin was well acquainted with the medieval concept of covenant as it related to anthropology, justification, and the sacraments.

Perhaps a short history lesson will help us here. Geerhardus Vos rightly notes: "The doctrine of the covenants is a peculiarly Reformed doctrine."[52] With the Reformation came a serious return to the study of Scripture using grammatical/historical/biblical hermeneutics, and the Swiss theologians in particular returned to the Bible's root idea of the preeminence of God's glory not only in creation but also in salvation. It was natural then that they would develop the biblical concept of the covenants as the instrumentalities whereby God determined to bring glory to himself by the salvation of the elect through the mediatorial work of his Son and the ministrations of his Spirit and Word. Covenant theology, then, emerged on Swiss soil, particularly in Geneva in Calvin's thought and in Zürich both in the writings of Zwingli, who in his debates with the Anabaptists made the covenant his main argument for the Reformed understanding of infant baptism, and in the sermons of Bullinger, his successor. Also in his *Of the One and Eternal Testament or Covenant of God*, the first treatise in church history on the covenant as such, Bullinger argues that the entirety of

---

[51]Peter A. Lillback, *The Binding of God: Calvin's Role in the Development of Covenant Theology* (Grand Rapids: Baker, 2001), 126.

[52]Geerhardus Vos, "The Doctrine of the Covenant in Reformed Theology," in *Redemptive History and Biblical Interpretation: The Shorter Writings of Geerhardus Vos*, 234.

Scripture must be viewed in the light of the Abrahamic covenant in which God graciously offers to give himself to men and in turn requires that men "walk before him and be perfect." Lillback argues that very little difference existed between Calvin and Bullinger in these regards: both maintained that God entered into a covenant of works (not fully developed in Calvin) with the pre-fall Adam, that after Adam's fall God's covenant relation with Adam's descendants became more defined through the process of progressive revelation, that the Abrahamic covenant is salvifically definitive for both the Old and New Testaments, and that the continuity between the Testaments counters the arguments of the Anabaptists.

The dual influence of the Geneva Reformer of French-speaking Switzerland and of the Zürich Reformers of German-speaking Switzerland in these regards was widespread and lasting. They influenced the Heidelberg theologians, Caspar Olevianus and Zacharias Ursinus, both men, as we noted earlier, having studied with Calvin in Geneva and both having spent some time in Zürich as well. Olevianus accordingly wrote *The Substance of the Covenant of Grace between God and the Elect* (1585), and Ursinus applied the covenant concept in his *Larger Catechism* (1612). Their ideas respectively of a pre-creation covenant between God the Father and God the Son for the salvation of the elect (the germ of which may be found in the *Institutes*, 3.21.5) and of a pre-fall covenant of law between God and man that promised life for perfect obedience and threatened death for disobedience (again, the germ of which may be found in the *Institutes*, 4.14.18), resulted in the developed covenant theology of such men as Cocceius.[53]

The Swiss Reformers also influenced the development of covenant theology in England. Many preachers and

---

[53]See Cocceius' *Summa doctrinae de foedere et testamento Dei* (1648).

scholars had fled to Geneva and Zürich during the reign of Queen Mary, and both Calvin and Bullinger maintained correspondence with them after they returned to England. Accordingly, Robert Rollock and Robert Howie in Scotland, Thomas Cartwright, John Preston, Thomas Blake, and John Ball in England, and James Ussher in Ireland all developed and wrote their theologies along covenantal lines. Bullinger's *Decades*, five books of ten long sermons each that were structured entirely by the covenant idea, were also translated into English in 1577 and made the official guide for clergy who had not obtained the master's degree. Influenced as they were by the labors of these men, the framers of the *Westminster Confession of Faith* placed the concept of the covenant in the foreground of their confessional deliverances, even giving creedal status to the covenant of works and the covenant of grace (see *Westminster Confession of Faith*, VII.2-6). While the influence of the confessional material of the Westminster Assembly was short-lived in England (the Savoy Declaration of 1658, a modification of the Westminster Confession to suit English congregational polity, was the exception here), being stifled by Charles II's restoration to the English throne in 1660, its *Confession of Faith* and *Catechisms* were adopted by the Church of Scotland and later by the Presbyterian churches in colonial America. And through these churches the covenant theology of the Westminster Assembly since the 1640s has had a growing influence over Protestant theology around the world, even in churches that have never formally adopted the Westminster documents as their own.

Consequently, a fair reading of all the facts will place Calvin squarely at the beginning of the Swiss Reformation's concept of covenant theology. He *was* seminally covenantal, then, in his theology; and his theology seminally contained essential covenantal elements.

c. In tone the *Institutes* is positivistic, that is, dogmatic. This is perhaps its prime offense in the eyes of its critics. Warfield writes:

> There is no mistaking the note of confidence in [Calvin's] teaching, and it is perhaps not surprising that this note of confidence irritates his critics. They resent the air of finality he gives to his declarations, not staying to consider that he gives them this air of finality because he presents them, not as his teachings, but as the teachings of the Holy Spirit in His inspired Word. Calvin's positiveness of tone is thus the mark not of extravagance but of sobriety and restraint...it was just because he refused to go one step beyond what is written that he felt so sure of his steps. He could not present the dictates of the Holy Ghost as a series of debatable propositions.[54]

It should be noted in this connection that Calvin's "positiveness" was often expressed in ways that we in this age, who have been reared on Dale Carnegie's *How to Win Friends and Influence People*, would regard as strident and acrimonious in the extreme. One could conclude if he did not know better that Calvin was a violent, mean, and hateful man, as his detractors often allege. Before one concludes this, however, he should recall that men of honor in that age, as well as the apostles in the New Testament age, believed there was virtue in speaking their minds very bluntly to one another.

d. The *Institutes* is rhetorical. By this I do not mean that it exhibits the rhetoric of scholasticism (the "art of reasoning") as much as it does the rhetoric of humanism (the "art of persuasion"). In this regard Calvin's Christian humanism influenced him in two ways as he wrote the *Institutes*: first, with respect to content, he goes back primarily to Scripture (*ad fontes*)—the genius of the Reformation principle of

---

[54]Warfield, "John Calvin the Theologian," *Calvin and Augustine*, 482.

sola scriptura—and he appeals, viewing them as secondary sources, to some forty church fathers, especially Augustine, not to mention about half that many classical authors. Second, with respect to style, he is persuasive as well as passionately demonstrative, using digression, repetition, wit, humor, sarcasm and other literary devices that add power to his point.

e. Finally, the work is pastoral. The title of the 1536 edition underscores this fact: *The Institute of the Christian Religion Containing Almost the Whole Sum of Piety and Whatever It is Necessary to Know in the Doctrine of Salvation.* In sum, from the outset Calvin was attempting to write, not a *summa theologica,* but a *summa pietatis.* One may recall here the motto of Calvin's life: "My heart I offer you, O Lord, promptly and sincerely"; that motto certainly is exhibited throughout the *Institutes* (see, for example, his "Life of the Christian," 3.7.1). This is because, for Calvin, "Piety is requisite for the knowledge of God" (*Institutes,* 1.2.1).

The 1559 edition reflects the pastoral experience he gained from his ministries in Strasbourg and Geneva as well as from his theological controversies with such men as Peter Caroli and Michael Servetus regarding the Trinity, with the Anabaptists regarding the place the Old Testament serves in the Christian life, and with the Lutherans and Zwinglians regarding issues pertaining to the Lord's Supper. Thus Calvin's *Institutes,* writes Ford Lewis Battles, is a "work of truly pastoral theology."[55]

Major Theological Contributions of the *Institutes*
We have time only to mention a few of the major contributions of the *Institutes* to theological thought:

---

[55]Ford Lewis Battles, *Analysis of the Institutes of the Christian Religion* (Grand Rapids: Baker, 1980; Reprint, Phillipsburg, N. J.: Presbyterian & Reformed, 2001), 14.

a. Its stress (1) on the Scriptures as the needed "spectacles" to read natural revelation aright (1.6.1; 1.14.1), the needed "thread through a labyrinth" to comprehend the divine countenance (1.6.3), and the needed "teacher" in order to understand "true religion" (1.6.2), and (2) on the "testimony of the Holy Spirit," the inner working of the Spirit of God in the sinner's heart in regeneration without which the revelation of God in the written Word, although intrinsically authoritative and self-authenticating (ˁστρμ;νγθρμλ, *autopiston*),[56] is spread before the sinner in vain (1.7.5).

b. Its stress on and defense of the Bible as *alone* the ground of all true knowledge of God (1.13.21).

c. Its doctrine of the Son and the Spirit as *autotheotic* (God of themselves) within the depths of the triune divine Being over against the assertions of some that they derive their divine essence from the Father through the *continuing* acts

---

[56]In the French version of the *Institutes* (1.7.5) Calvin writes at this point that Scripture "carries with itself its [own] credentials" (*porte avec soi sa créance*). A careful reading of the next chapter (1.8), that in my opinion would have been better titled, "Evidences from Scripture for Scripture's Credibility," will show that Calvin is in the main presenting biblical data in favor of the Bible's authenticity and truthfulness. Virtually all of his arguments for the credibility of Scripture (the "heavenly character of its doctrine," its "very heavenly majesty," "the beautiful agreement of all the parts," its "incontestable miracles" and "confirmed prophecy") are drawn from the Bible. What little evidence he adduces that is not drawn from Scripture (the indestructibility of Scripture through the ages, its wide acceptance by the nations, the willingness of martyrs to die for it) in 1.8.12, 13 is not the main thrust of this much-discussed chapter and frankly is not compelling since the same could be said of other books such as the Koran. To the degree that Calvin used these external evidences for the authenticity and truthfulness of Scripture, to that same degree in my opinion he compromised his own *sola Scriptura* principle.

respectively of the Father's eternal begetting of the Son and the Father's eternal processing of the Spirit out of himself (1.13.19-25).[57] This Calvin thought "foolish" (1.13.29).

d. Its stress on the continuity between Old and New Testament salvation (2.9-11),[58] becoming as a result a seminal source of covenant theology.

e. Its treatment of Christ's work under the rubric of his three-fold office of Prophet, Priest, and King (2.15-17).

f. Its development throughout, but particularly in Book Three, of the doctrine of the work of the Holy Spirit—certainly one of its greatest theological contributions.

g. Its advocacy of the Protestant doctrine of justification by faith alone, Calvin declaring this doctrine to be "the main hinge on which religion turns,"[59] "the sum of all of piety,"[60] and the "first and keenest subject of controversy"[61] between Rome and the Reformation.

---

[57] Pope Leo I declared the later doctrine of the "double procession" of the Spirit from the Father *and the Son* (the *filioque*) to be an aspect of the orthodox faith and the Third Council of Toledo in A.D. 589 gave it conciliar authority. Benjamin B. Warfield in "John Calvin the Theologian," *Calvin and Augustine*, 483, argues that Calvin's doctrine of the autotheotic nature of the Son and the Spirit "marked an epoch in the history of the doctrine of the Trinity." For a fuller discussion of this contribution see my *A New Systematic Theology of the Christian Faith* (Second edition; Nashville, Tennessee: Thomas Nelson, 2002), 323-35.

[58] For my argument for the unity of Old and New Testament salvation, see my *A New Systematic Theology of the Christian Faith* (Second edition; Nashville, Tennessee: Thomas Nelson, 2002), 503-44.

[59] Calvin, *Institutes of the Christian Religion*, 3.11.1.

[60] Calvin, *Institutes of the Christian Religion*, 3.11.1.

[61] Calvin, "Reply to Sadoleto," *A Reformation Debate* (Grand Rapids: Baker, 1966), 66. He asserts in this same context: "...wherever

h. Its doctrine of predestination—simply his restatement of Augustine's teaching on predestination, sin, and grace, or rather, to be more precise, a restatement of the Bible's teaching on predestination, sin, and grace—in which the will of God is the "primary cause" of all things, both good and evil (3.21-24).

We need to underscore here this connection between the Augustinian and Calvinistic systems in church history. What we know today as sixteenth-century "Calvinism" was *essentially and simply a purer restatement of fifth-century Augustinianism eleven centuries later!* In the fifth century the truths on predestination, sin, and grace that Augustine preached and taught—or rather, to be more correct, the truths on predestination, sin, and grace in the Word of God for which Augustine had contended—had ultimately triumphed over Pelagianism and even semi-Pelagianism and reigned supreme in the church until the doctrinal decline of the church buried the fruit of Augustine's labors completely out of sight and mind, just as the church's decline since the days of the Reformation has buried to a major degree the fruit of Calvin's labors. We must pray to God that he will not allow eleven more centuries to pass before the church as a whole again embraces these God-exalting doctrines!

i. Its insistence (4.12) that the discipline of the sinning saint resides in the hands of the church's ministers and not in the

---

the knowledge of [this doctrine] is taken away, the glory of Christ is extinguished, religion abolished, the Church destroyed, and the hope of salvation utterly overthrown." Reformed pastors who follow today the teaching of Norman Shepherd and N.T. Wright need to heed Calvin's words here! For when conformity to a legal standard is alleged to be *the* "Lutheran" error, and when justifying "righteousness" is regarded as covenant faithfulness, as these two teachers allege, those who buy into their "catholicizing" of the doctrine need to realize they are doing precisely what Calvin opposes here.

hands of the magistrate (by which insistence Calvin gave utterance to what came to be known later as "the crown rights of King Jesus in his church"). This insistence ultimately emancipated the church from the state and the state from the church. Thus by his unique program of *church* discipline "Calvin became nothing less than the creator of the Protestant Church."

A related topic is Calvin's view on church government.[62] Over against the prelatical view of church government that had prevailed with little resistance throughout the Middle Ages and that resulted finally in all the doctrinal errors and moral evils of the Roman Papacy, Calvin, as one aspect of his effort to return the church to its scriptural moorings, eventually instituted in the four churches in Geneva, on the basis of his understanding of the ministry of the Word as fourfold (namely, the pastor, the doctor or teacher, the elder, and the deacon), the Presbyterian form of church government, with the churches there having authority, as we have already noted, over the ministry of the Word, the administration of the sacraments, and the discipline of its members independent of that city-state's authority (4.3-7).

While his was not the full-blown Presbyterianism we see today, lacking as it did at least one upper court, Calvin's efforts laid the foundation for it,[63] and accordingly Presby-

---

[62]See my article, 'Presbyterian Church Government,' in *Perspectives on Church Government, Five Views of Church Polity*, edited by Stan Norman and Chad Brand (Nashville: Broadman and Holman, 2004).

[63]French Protestants secretly meeting in Paris in 1559 officially organized a French Reformed Church in which Presbyterian polity was set up, beginning with the lowest judicatories of local church consistories composed of representative elders, then middle or regional judicatories composed of representative elders from the consistories of the several districts, and finally the highest judicatory, that is, the national synod made up of elders from the regional presbyteries.

terianism spread from Geneva and developed in Switzerland, Germany, France, South Africa, the Netherlands, Scotland, Northern Ireland, and Wales; and then from these European countries, specially from Britain and the Netherlands, Presbyterianism spread to the New World where it became very influential in the original American colonies and the Great Awakening. Then through the great missionary movement in the nineteenth century, Presbyterian missionaries carried Presbyterianism far and wide, and national Presbyterian churches were founded in many parts of the world. That same Presbyterian missionary labor continues to the present time.

j. Its major treatment on civil government (4.20) that makes room for both Church and State as from God and standing in a *cooperative* relation with each other and both worthy of obedience. Calvin provides no place in the State either for a supreme emperor or for clerical domination. Rather, he argues for the idea of "mutual obligation" between the ruler and the ruled and makes political resistance against imperial tyranny a calling and obligation only of the lesser magistrates of the people (in his last years Calvin appears to have developed a stronger theory of resistance than interposition only by the lesser magistrates, appealing to the "private law" theory that held that individuals may resist the tyranny of the civil magistrate). He seems to have favored a representative or aristocratic republican form of civil government subordinate to the Word of God.

Calvin appears to give place in his political philosophy to what is called today "natural law theory," but in my opinion his "natural law" should be associated not so much with a brute "rational operation" but with the voice of conscience.[64]

---

[64]For this distinction I am indebted to Mark Édouward Chenevière, *La pensée politique de Calvin* (Geneva, 1937).

Because Calvin taught that the Holy Spirit enables the magistrate, Josef Bohatec suggests that Calvin's political philosophy of the State should more precisely be regarded as "pneumatocratic" than "theocratic."[65]

k. Its creative contribution to what has come to be called "Christian vocation" and the "Protestant work ethic" that maintains (1) that the laborer should see his vocation and labor as a divine calling, (2) that no legitimate labor is in itself demeaning, and (3) that therefore even the lowliest laborer has dignity as he fulfils his calling.[66]

l. Its general, overall theological depiction of Christianity (1) as Theism come into its own, (2) as Religion at the height of its conception, and (3) as Evangelicalism in its purest and most stable expression.

We have highlighted only some of the more significant accomplishments of Calvin's second Geneva period. We have time now only to mention some specific events and dates during the period now under discussion.

SOME SPECIFIC EVENTS AND DATES

Calvin's only son, Jacques, was born July 28, 1542 but lived only a few days. Heartbroken, Calvin wrote to Peter Viret:

[65]Josef Bohatec, "Die Souveranität Gottes und der Staat nach der Auffassung Calvins," Second International Calvin Congress, 71-106. For a helpful bibliography on Calvin's political views I would recommend John T. McNeill's "Fifty Years of Calvin Study," to be found in Williston Walker's *John Calvin*, xlviii-liii, lxxvi-lxvii.

[66]A helpful article here is C. Gregg Singer's "Calvin and the Social Order," to be found in *John Calvin: Contemporary Prophet*, edited by Jacob T. Hoogstra (Philadelphia: Presbyterian and Reformed, 1959), 227-41. For a helpful bibliography on Calvin's view of the Christian life and the "Protestant work ethic" I would recommend John T. McNeill's "Fifty Years of Calvin Study," to be found in Williston Walker's *John Calvin*, xlv-xlviii, lxxv-lxxvi.

"The Lord has certainly inflicted a severe and bitter wound in the death of our baby son, but he is himself a Father and knows what is good for his children."

In 1543 he published his *Reply to Albertus Pighius* in which he defended Luther and with him opposed the Catholic doctrine of free will. He returned to this debate in 1552 with his treatise, *Concerning the Eternal Predestination of God.*

The counter-Reformation Council of Trent convened in December 1545. With the prospects of a Catholic renewal facing Protestantism, Calvin was spurred anew to bring Lutherans, Zwinglians, and his own followers into a united Protestantism. He hammered out a document in 1549 with Heinrich Bullinger, known as the "Zürich Consensus," that affirmed the spiritual presence of Christ in the Lord's Supper. He had high hopes that Melanchthon, representing Lutheranism, would sign on to it, but the tired and always somewhat timid Melanchthon as well as the anti-Melanchthonians within Lutheranism, refused to accept it. So completely did Lutheran rigorists, such as Joachim Westphal and Tilemann Heshusius, control the Lutheran churches by this time that when Calvin visited Strasbourg in 1557 he was not allowed to preach in the churches. Calvin also supported the effort of England's Archbishop Cranmer and Archbishop Parker to convene a meeting of Protestant leaders to promote the consolidation of the churches of the Reformation. But because of Cranmer's martyrdom nothing ever came of the effort.

When Martin Luther died in 1546, from that point on Calvin more and more was looked to as the major leader of the Reformation cause, with Protestant leaders and sympathizers from all the countries of Europe streaming almost daily to Geneva (and to Idelette's hospitable supper table) to seek his opinions and advice on many and diverse church matters.

That same year he also translated Melanchthon's *Loci theologici* into French and wrote a preface to it.

Accepting his responsibility as the major leader of the Reformation cause, in November 1547 Calvin published his *Antidote* to the *Acts of the Council of Trent* formulated in that council's first seven sessions, in which he showed that the heresies of Rome are numerous and deadly.[67]

After a protracted illness Idelette died in 1549. Calvin remained a widower the remaining fifteen years of his life. Again writing to his friend Peter Viret shortly after her death Calvin said:

> I have been bereaved of the best companion of my life, who, if our lot had been harsher, would have been not only the willing sharer of exile and poverty, but even of death. While she lived, she was the faithful helper of my ministry. From her I never experienced the slightest hindrance.

Time requires that we leave Calvin now, as we just said, as a bereaved widower, but unlike the condition in which we left him in our second lecture—exiled from Geneva and without ministerial call—we leave him now at the height of his intellectual powers and as the most significant and influential, the most-widely revered and respected, and the most sought-after Protestant leader in all Europe.

---

[67]Calvin's *Antidote* may be found in *Selected Works of John Calvin: Tracts and Letters*, edited and translated by Henry Beveridge (Reprint; Grand Rapids: Baker, 1983), 3, 17-188.

CHAPTER FOUR

THE BURNING OF SERVETUS AND THE REFORMER'S LAST YEARS

At the end of our last lecture we left Calvin carrying out his divine calling in Geneva as the most significant, the most sought-after Reformation leader in all Europe, and as the founder of the Protestant church.

THE BURNING OF MICHAEL SERVETUS

I want to begin this final lecture by addressing head-on the one blot on Calvin's ministry for which his memory, above any other deed he did, is reviled today by his enemies and by those who know only what they have been told about him. That event is Geneva's burning of Michael Servetus. This topic will occupy the first portion of this final lecture. We will then bring our lecture series to a close by fleshing out the accomplishments of Calvin's last years.

Michael Servetus, the arch-heretic of Calvin's day, was born September 29, 1511. A Spanish physician, he had a brilliant mind for medicine (he discovered the so-called lesser circulation of the blood) but became more and more involved in theological controversy. Believing that he was one with the "Michael" in the Book of Revelation fighting against both the dragon of Rome and the "Simon Magus" or "magician" of Geneva and thus destined to "reform" both the papacy and the Reformation, in his two books, *On the Errors of the Trinity* (1531) and *The Restitution of Christianity* (1533), he denied the doctrine of the Trinity and the deity of Christ, declaring that in the place of God the church had substituted a Cerberus with three heads (which

111

denials placed him in the ranks of the blasphemer) and rejected infant baptism (which rejection placed him in the thinking of many among the Anabaptists who were regularly persecuted for this rejection).

In spite of exhausting, time-consuming labor on Calvin's part to convert him from his error through correspondence, Servetus rejected all of the well-intended efforts of Calvin who finally broke off all communication with him. For some unknown reason[1] Servetus entered Geneva and was arrested on August 13, 1553, tried, and burned at the stake on the hill called Champel at the south gate of Geneva on October 27 that same year.[2] Calvin, being the leading Protestant theologian of the city, was the chief prosecution witness (Claude Rigot being the chief prosecutor) against him at his heresy trial.[3] Calvin's involvement in Servetus' trial has become the darkest blot for many on Calvin's reputation, and his involvement in Servetus' execution has for many

---

[1]Wolfgang Musculus (1497-1563), a Reformed pastor from Lorraine who ended his life ministering in Berne, explaining the affair later to Bullinger, maintained that Servetus' coming to Geneva was part of a gigantic conspiracy: "Servetus recently came to Geneva to take advantage of the rancor felt toward Calvin by the government."

[2]Theodore Beza observed that in his dying prayer Servetus cried: "O Jesus, son of eternal God, have pity on me." Had he only prayed: "O Jesus, eternal Son of God," his prayer would have been orthodox. His punishment was due to his misplacing a single adjective, but "heresy is often just a question of grammar" (Cottret).

[3]Some historians have attributed to Calvin motives that are less than pure to explain his willingness to be as deeply involved as he was in Servetus' prosecution, urging that by seeing Servetus condemned Calvin was attempting, first, to furnish proof of his own Trinitarian orthodoxy against the charge of Arianism that Peter Caroli had made against him over fifteen years before, and, second, to bring authority and respectability to the Genevan church. Calvin himself believed he was simply carrying out the will of God regarding the punishment of heretics as he understood God's will as expressed in Holy Scripture.

undone all the good for which Calvin might otherwise have been credited. What shall we say about this tragic event in Calvin's life? Can anything be said that will temper the judgment of the world against the Genevan reformer for his part in Servetus' execution by burning?

William Cunningham lists the following five considerations that ameliorate to some degree Calvin's involvement in Servetus' execution:

1. The doctrine of not only the lawfulness but also the duty of putting heretics and blasphemers to death was then almost universally held by Protestants as well as Roman Catholics. That is to say, the Genevan authorities and Calvin the Reformer were hardly alone in this respect regarding the execution of heretics. Conventional church wisdom endorsed the executions of those whose doctrine could mislead the masses and put them on the broad road that leads to destruction.[4]

2. Servetus was not only a heretic and a blasphemer but one who did everything to provoke and nothing to conciliate. For example, so defiant was he before the Little Council during his trial that he demanded that Calvin, whom he

---

[4]The reason that the execution of heretics was a commonplace in that day Abraham Kuyper explains in the following way in his *Lectures on Calvinism* (Grand Rapids: Eerdmans, 1931), 100:

The duty of the government to extirpate every form of false religion and idolatry was not a find of Calvinism, but dates from Constantine the Great, and was the reaction against the horrible persecutions which his pagan predecessors on the imperial throne had inflicted upon the sect of the Nazarene. Since that day this system had been defended by all Romish theologians and applied by all Christian princes. In the time of Luther and Calvin, it was a universal conviction that that system was the true one.

continually labeled before the Council as a liar, a false accuser, an imposter, a miserable wretch, a hypocrite, and an ignorant calumniator, be imprisoned according to the *lex talionis* (law of retaliation) and that Calvin's property be awarded to him in the event that the Council determined to put Calvin to death rather than him. At this last request even the Council members could not retain their seriousness, for Calvin's utter poverty was a proverb throughout the city and indeed beyond the city walls.[5]

3. Servetus had already been convicted of heresy and blasphemy by a papal tribunal at Vienne, France and had already been condemned to be burned at the stake by slow fire. He escaped from the Vienne authorities and came to Geneva with that sentence hanging over his head. Therefore, the civil authorities at Geneva feared that the papal authorities would have grounds to charge them and Protestantism in general with being indifferent, if not favorable, to heresy if they spared him.

4. Although Calvin undoubtedly approved of putting Servetus to death as an incorrigible heretic and blasphemer, he exerted all of his ministerial influence on the Little Council, although unsuccessfully, to prevent Servetus from being executed by burning, urging that he be executed by some less cruel means such as decapitation by the sword. So all the talk one hears about Calvin burning Servetus, so prevalent today, is simply and literally a blatant misrepresentation. Calvin did not burn Servetus. Indeed, he was opposed to his execution by burning.

---

[5]"The strength of that heretic consisted in this," said Pope Pius IV, hearing of Calvin's death, "that money never had the slightest charm for him. If I had such servants my dominion would extend from sea to sea" (Philip Schaff, *History of the Christian Church*, VIII, 839).

5. The Protestant cities of Zürich, Basel, Schaffhausen, and Berne were polled before the Council determined to execute Servetus and they unanimously replied that they regarded him as a heretic, though they did not specify his punishment since they did not want to intrude upon the authority of the Genevan magistracy. And two of the mildest and most moderate of the major Reformed leaders—Melanchthon representing the Lutherans and Bullinger representing the Zwinglians—after Servetus' execution gave their full, formal, and public approbation to the proceedings that had taken place in Geneva. So it was apparent that all of Swiss Protestantism was supportive of Calvin's prosecution of and the Genevan magistracy's execution of Servetus.[6] Even Calvin's chief enemy at the time, Jérome-Hermès Bolsec, expressed satisfaction at the death of "such a monstrous heretic who was so evil and unworthy to live."[7]

Cunningham concludes that "all that Calvin ever said or did in the case of Servetus, is fully explained by his conviction of the lawfulness and duty of putting heretics and blasphemers to death; and by his uncompromising determination to maintain, in every way he regarded lawful, the interests of God's truth, and to discharge his own obligations."[8]

I would like to add some further details and thoughts of my own (eight points, to be specific) by way of elaboration to Cunningham's five:

1. Students of Calvin's life must clearly perceive and keep ever before them that Servetus' execution by fire was decided

---

[6]William Cunningham, "John Calvin," in *The Reformers and the Theology of the Reformation* (Reprint; London: Banner of Truth, 1967), 318-22.

[7]See Appedix A for Bolsec's opinion of Calvin.

[8]Cunningham, "John Calvin," in *The Reformers and the Theology of the Reformation*, 322.

by the *secular* Little Council, the majority of whose members at this time were *opposed* to Calvin's entire ministry, and not by Calvin who admittedly did desire his conviction and death and who appeared as chief prosecution witness against him. But even as his chief opponent Calvin loaned Servetus from his own library whatever ancient books he requested for the preparation of his defense.

In actuality, Calvin was not a citizen of the city of Geneva and therefore could not have stood for political office if he had desired to do so, could not have voted in city elections had he wanted to, and therefore could not have voted in judicial matters and certainly *did not vote* to execute Servetus by fire.

2. During his trial the Little Council gave Servetus the opportunity to be extradited back to Vienne, France. Having been given reason to think that the Libertines on the Little Council were going to find in his favor against Calvin, he begged the Council with tears not to extradite him, so the trial continued in Geneva. The Council, once it determined to continue to oversee the trial, had really only two major penalties it could impose in order to avoid the charge of being soft on heresy: either banishment or execution. But, as Cunningham notes, because Servetus was already under the sentence of death at Vienne, banishment was simply not regarded as a real option in his case.

3. Calvin, as has been said, and the Venerable Company of ministers were opposed to the idea of Geneva imitating Rome with a burning of a heretic on Genevan soil and tried to convince the Council, but to no avail, that the fire penalty for heresy, that by the way had been outlawed in Geneva by Calvin's *Ordinances* of 1542, was a hangover from old Catholic canon law and was neither required by Scripture nor authorized by Geneva's own law.

4. It is only my opinion but had Calvin's plea been heard and had Servetus been executed by the headman's axe instead of by fire, little fuss would have been made of it then (or perhaps even now). I say this for good reason. How many today have heard of Jacques Gruet? Very few, I am sure. Well, Jacques Gruet, a citizen of Geneva and an enemy of Calvin, on June 27, 1547 was alleged to have hung a placard on the pulpit of St. Peter's Church on which he threatened the lives of the Genevan preachers. He was tried by the magistracy, condemned to death, and beheaded. Nothing much, if anything, is said today about this execution in Geneva. Of course, burnings in Catholic countries and beheadings in Lutheran countries (for example, the beheading at Leipzig in 1601 of Nicholas Crellius, the Calvinist chancellor of Christian I) commonly took place because of offenses judged to be heresies. Cardinal Torquemada, the leader of the Spanish Inquisition, in his eighteen years in office burned alive, it is estimated, around eight thousand, eight hundred people and tortured around ninety thousand other people on the rack and in various others ways, not for offenses against the moral law of God or for crimes against society but simply for their anti-Catholic views. And mass executions occurred in Germany after the Peasants' War (1525) and after the ending of the siege of Münster (1534). In England in 1549 Archbishop Cranmer succeeded in having two convicted heretics burned at the stake whose offenses were far less aggravating than Servetus' blasphemies. In fact, at the behest of the bishops of London and Lichfield, as late as 1612, the English secular arm burned two individuals whose views were similar to Servetus' views. But does anyone say anything about or hear about these executions today? No. It is this *one* stake, taken over from Rome by a Protestant secular counsel, a stake by the way that the Reformed world deplores, that has become the primary cause of the

vilification of Calvin's memory and of all his labor. Where is any semblance of judicious balance in all this?

5. While the burning of even one heretic is one burning too many, at least it should be noted that never did Geneva ever burn one Roman Catholic for his faith, something that the Roman Church cannot say about its treatment of Protestants. In fact, Servetus was the *only* individual burned for his religious views in Geneva during Calvin's entire time there, at a time, as we have already said, when executions of this nature were a commonplace almost everywhere else in Europe.

6. When all the facts surrounding this event are considered, it would appear that there is as good, if not better, evidence that those who denounce Calvin hate him as that Calvin hated Servetus and plotted his death.[9] And why do his defamers so strongly detest Calvin? I would suggest, most likely because they cannot abide his God-centered theological system and its demanding moral requirements! For if Servetus' execution

---

[9]Edward Gibbon, for example, writes in his *Decline and Fall of the Roman Empire* (Smith edition), V, chapter 14, 552 fn: "I am more deeply scandalized at the single execution of Servetus than at the hecatombs which have blazed at Auto-da-fés of Spain and Portugal." Why such terribly unjust and unbalanced prejudice in the judgment of this eighteenth-century historian? Because, Gibbon says—among other equally bad reasons—Calvin violated the Golden Rule! As if the Romanist persecutors had kept it!

Wallace, the Unitarian, in his *Anti-Trinitarian Biography* (3 volumes; 1850), 1, 442-6, writes: "A bloodier page does not stain the annals of martyrdom than that in which this horrible transaction is recorded...." Calvin's prosecutorial role stamps Calvin's character, he declares, as that "of a persecutor of the first class, without one humane or redeeming quality to divest it of its criminality or to palliate its enormity...[as] one of the foulest murders recorded in the history of persecution."

had occurred in any Catholic country in Europe at the hands of Catholic authorities it would have been just one more "puff of smoke," just one more of thousands of such stakes that were continually being set on fire in Spain, France, the Netherlands, the England of "bloody Mary," and the Scotland of Cardinal James Beaton—fired, I would remind you, to remove those who were in the main the followers of biblical doctrine—and nothing much today would be said about it. But because Servetus was burned in this one Protestant city, and particularly because of Calvin's involvement in his trial, much is made of it today in a negative way. I have already stated that even one burning anywhere is one burning too many and that Calvin can never be completely exonerated for his part in Servetus' execution "unless [one is] prepared to defend the lawfulness of putting heretics to death."[10] But there should be *some* sense of proportion in any assessment *today* of Servetus' execution *then*. It is simply unfair to single Calvin out as if he were the *originator* of the practice of burning heretics or as if he were a particularly violent supporter of the practice at a time when a vast majority of the European continent's enlightened populace would have wished it were otherwise.[11] The simple truth of the matter is that Calvin was opposed to execution by burning.

7. The Servetus case involved a lot more in the Genevan situation than simply the trial of one man for his heresies. It

---

[10]Cunningham, "John Calvin," 316.

[11]Abraham Kuyper also speaks of the "unfairness" that secular and church historians have exhibited toward Calvin because of his involvement in the burning of Servetus in his *Lectures on Calvinism*, 100:

…whilst the Calvinists, in the age of Reformation, yielded their victims, by tens of thousands, to the scaffold and the stake…, history has been guilty of the great and far-reaching unfairness of ever casting in their teeth this one execution of fire of Servetus, as a *crimen nefandum.*

became the *cause célèbre* that was to test the relative strengths of the competing socio/political powers vying for the ascendency in Geneva at the time. Calvin's enemies on the Little Council (Ami Perrin and Philibert Berthelier), perceiving that Servetus' conviction would strengthen Calvin's hand, tried several maneuvers in order to acquit Servetus but failed in their efforts. From their perspective, Calvin's involvement in Servetus' trial contributed much more ideologically to their acquittal of Servetus than to his condemnation. But their efforts to rescue Servetus seem to have only hardened Calvin in his pursuit of Servetus to the death. And after Servetus' execution, when Protestant leaders unanimously supported Servetus' conviction and expressed their appreciation to Calvin for Geneva's having rid the world of Servetus, his reputation throughout the Reformed world was only enhanced. Heinrich Bullinger at Zürich expressed his approval; Philip Melanchthon declared that Calvin had earned the gratitude not only of the whole church but of all posterity (little did *he* know!); Johann Haller at Berne said that Servetus had received his just reward; Wolfgang Musculus commended the execution in elegant verse which he sent to his colleague, Ambrosius Blaurer, at Basel; and Peter Martyr called Servetus "a child of the devil" and declared that Geneva had done its work well.

Quite soon thereafter, the Genevan citizenry that had swelled in number due to the influx of French refugees into the city, most of whom favored Calvin's reforms, voted the Perrinists out of power. This in turn gave the Genevan magistracy the political character by which Calvin finally saw his desire brought to fruition for a system of church discipline independent of the State that would eventually mean in turn, "No more burnings!" Once again, *Post Tenebras Lux!*

8. Finally, a fact little known today is that there now stands a granite monument near the site where Servetus was

burned—inspired not by his opponents but by Émile Doumergue, one of Calvin's greatest admirers and his most significant biographer—paid for by Reformed and Presbyterian church bodies in Switzerland, the Netherlands, France, Britain, and North America and erected on the three hundred and fiftieth anniversary of Servetus' burning.[12] It bears two inscriptions. The first one reads in translation from the French:

> On the 27th of October 1553 died at the stake at Champel Michael Servet from Villeneuve, Aragon, born on the 29th of September 1511.

The second, on the other side of the granite slab, reads:

> We, the respectful and thankful sons of Calvin, the Great Reformer, condemning an error, which was the error of the age in which Calvin lived,[13] and valuing above all things Liberty of Conscience according to the true doctrines of the Reformation and the Gospel, erected this monument of repentance on the 27th of October 1903.

On that occasion Doumergue spoke, and in his speech he suggested that Rome should erect a similar monument of repentance expressing sorrow for the massacres of St. Bartholomew's Day.

---

[12]First on the list of contributors to the cost of the monument was the Consistory of the Reformed Church of Geneva.

[13]This "error, which was the error of the age" Abraham Kuyper condemned, with Calvinists universally, in the following words in his *Lectures on Calvinism*, 100.

> ...I not only deplore that one stake, but I unconditionally disapprove of it; yet not as if it were the expression of a special characteristic of Calvinism, but on the contrary as the fatal after-effect of a system, gray with age, which Calvinism found in existence, under which it had grown up, and from which it had not yet been able to liberate itself.

For those who have little or no familiarity with the St. Bartholomew's Day massacres, time will not permit me to offer more than a couple of paragraphs about them. In 1572 a large number of Huguenot notables had come to Paris to attend the wedding of Henry of Navarre to the sister of King Charles IX. Catherine de Medici, the queen mother, conspired with Charles to have them killed. At the pre-established signal on August 24, Parisian Catholics roamed through the streets of Paris killing around two thousand French Protestants, and over a short time around twenty thousand other Huguenots in other large French cities were also massacred. When he heard the news, Pope Gregory XIII rejoiced and ordered thanksgiving services and the ringing of church bells in all the churches.

Incidentally, in 1868, two years before Vatican I, one of the greatest Roman Catholic historians of the nineteenth century, John Emerich Edward Dalberg, better known to the world as Lord Acton,[14] who coined the oft-quoted warning: "Power tends to corrupt; absolute power corrupts absolutely" (it is not commonly known by those who are familiar with his warning that Lord Acton was directing it not only against kings but also against the papacy), published a long essay in the *North British Review* about the massacres. He concluded:

> The story is much more abominable that we all believed.... S.B. is the greatest crime of modern times. It was committed on principles professed by Rome. It was approved, sanctioned, and praised by the papacy. The Holy See went out of its way to signify to the world, by permanent and solemn acts, how entirely it admired a king who slaughtered his subjects treacherously, because they were Protestants, to proclaim forever that because a man is a Protestant it is a pious deed to cut his throat in the night.[15]

---

[14]I am indebted to John W. Robbins' *Ecclesiastical Megalomania* for alerting me to the cited statements of Lord Acton.

By the way, Rome's expiatory monument is yet to be erected, for to do so would condemn the attitudes and actions of a reputedly holy Pope.

In concluding my discussion of the Servetus matter, may I point out that with reference to this acknowledged "error, which was the error of the age," a difference between the consensus of church leaders in the sixteenth century and the consensus of people in our "enlightened" secularistic age obviously exists about such a punishment. Modern "enlightened sensitivities" have led many in our time not only to fault the punishments of medieval times but also to reject capital punishment entirely as well as the Bible's doctrine of hell. But what about death by stoning which the following Old Testament verses clearly enjoin for blaspheming God's name and for similar offenses?

Leviticus 24:16: "He who blasphemes the name of the Lord shall be put to death; all the congregation shall stone him."

Deuteronomy 13:1-11: "If a prophet arises among you, or a dreamer of dreams..., and if he says: 'Let us go after other gods...,' you shall not yield to him or listen to him, nor shall your eye pity him, nor shall you spare him, nor shall you conceal him; but you shall kill him.... You shall stone him to death with stones, because he sought to draw you away from the Lord your God."

Were *these* biblical instructions "an error of that age"? The same people who condemn Calvin today would doubtless say yes, for our current "enlightened" imagination shudders at the terror and agony that victims of such punishments must have experienced. However, we who believe that the Bible is God's inspired Word must say no. These instructions were

[15]Lord Acton, Add. MSS 5004; cited by Gertrude Himmelfarb, *Lord Acton: A Study in Conscience and Politics* (Chicago: University Press, 1952), 67.

not "an error of that age." They were laws prescribed by God
himself for the training of his people and for the protection
of the pure religion under the old dispensation. Perhaps the
world would still be doing so had not the Second Person of
the Godhead, the giver of that Old Testament legislation, in
the person of Jesus Christ rescinded them himself for this
age by his and his apostles' later teaching (John 8:3-11;
1 Cor 5:11-13). As the *Westminster Confession of Faith*
declares:

> To [the nation of Israel], as a body politick, he gave sundry judicial
> laws, which expired together with the state of that people, not
> obliging any other now, further than the general equity thereof
> may require. (XIX/4)

But clearly in the sixteenth century the sense of order for
both Catholics and Protestants was horrified by something
else—something quite sobering and something to which few
in our day give heed anymore at all—namely, the thought of
immortal souls being destroyed by false doctrine, of
churches being rent asunder by heretical parties, and of God's
vengeance being poured out upon cities and nations that
tolerate and endorse immorality by means of war, pestilence,
and famine (see Psalm 2).

Which age is the more biblical, the more theologically
sensitive, the more enlightened? Theirs then or ours now?
You must judge whether our sensitivities today have proven
to be more beneficial, over all, for the spiritual state and
morals of mankind than theirs—sensitivities, by the way,
that are quite obviously much more comfortable criticizing
what are viewed as the "gross insensitivities" of sixteenth-
century executions of some thousands of heretics, that I
concur should never have been done by either Catholics or
Protestants, than dealing squarely with our insensitivities
to the legislative errors, in the name of secular humanist

human rights, of our own time, namely, the legalization of homosexuality as simply a variant, not a deviant, life style and the wanton *barbaric* abortion industry that has aborted over forty million infants in the U.S.A. alone on no other ground than the federal Supreme Court's determination that the Fourteenth Amendment of the United States Constitution gives a mother, completely apart from the father's wishes, the supposed "pro-choice right" over the offspring in her womb to decide whether the baby lives or dies. You must be the judge!

THE REFORMER'S LAST YEARS

We turn now, only briefly, to an overview of a few remaining activities in Calvin's last years.

The Little Council and the Council of Two Hundred finally ratified on January 24, 1555 the Consistory's right to ban impenitent church members from the Lord's Table, that is, the Consistory's right to wield the spiritual sword in its own domain, which right Calvin had been demanding since 1536, for which demand he had been banished in 1538, and for which he had been willing to jeopardize his entire professional career.

As we saw in our third lecture, Calvin finally saw the definitive Latin edition of his *Institutes* published in 1559, about which finished *theology* of this edition Williston Walker of Yale University writes:

> ...its value in the progress of Christian thought is not to be minimized or forgotten. It laid a profound emphasis on Christian intelligence. Its appeal was primarily to the intellect, and it has trained a sturdy race of thinkers on the problems of the faith wherever it has gone. It has been the foe of popular ignorance, and of shallow, emotional, or sentimental views of Christian faith. Equally significant as an educative force has been its insistence on the individual nature of

salvation. A personal relation of each man to God, a definite divine plan for each life, a value for the humblest individual in the God-appointed ordering of the universe, are thoughts which, however justly the social rather than the individual aspects of Christianity are now being emphasized, have demonstrated their worth in Christian history. Yet perhaps the crowning historic significance of Calvinism is to be seen in its valuation of character. Its conception of duty to know and do the will of God, not, indeed, as a means of salvation, but as that for which we are elected to life, and as the fitting tribute to the "honour of God" which we are bound to maintain, has made of the Calvinist always a representative of a strenuous morality. In this respect Calvin's system has been a tonic in the blood, and its educative effects are to be traced in the lands in which it has held sway even among those who have departed widely from his habit of thought. The spiritual indebtedness of western Europe and of North America to the educative influence of Calvin's theology is well-nigh measureless.[16]

Ford Lewis Battles, translator of Calvin's *Institutes* in *The Library of Christian Classics*, would enjoin his students as they commenced their study of the *Institutes*:

> You are about to share in one of the classic experiences of Christian history…on the deceptively orderly and seemingly dispassionate pages that follow are imprinted one man's passionate responses to the call of Christ. If [you] keep ever before [you] that autobiographical character of the book, the whole man will speak to [you] in very truth.[17]

Battles also cautioned with regard to reading the completed *Institutes*:

> First, you must want to read the book; second, you must set out *from the beginning*; third, you must persist, however long it takes

---

[16]Williston Walker, *John Calvin*, 428.

[17]Ford Lewis Battles, *Analysis of the Institutes* (Phillipsburg, N.J.: Presbyterian and Reformed, 2001), 14.

you, until you reach the last page. Do not become a Calvinist of the first five chapters or of the first book. I can generally tell, when people speak of Calvin, whether they know him only by hearsay, have read a few pages, or have sampled him anthologically. They have no clue to the wonderful interconnectedness of Calvin's thought. They ask questions which a fuller reading of the *Institutes* could have answered. Fourth, do not lament that a question seems to go unanswered, or a loose end seems not to be tied: it will be answered; it will be tied. Be patient. If, after you have read the whole book for the first time, you remain in serious disagreement with Calvin—well, so be it! But what coherent alternative will you have to offer? Fifth, as you read, think not only of Calvin's time...but also of our own. Is Calvin somehow speaking too to the late twentieth century? So speculating, readers of the *Institutes* have sometimes made surprisingly helpful discoveries.

So much for Calvin's *opus magnum*, his *Institutes*—the most influential systematic theology ever written. Time constraints insist that we press ahead.

That same year (1559) Calvin wrote the *French Confession of Faith* (*Confessio Fidei Gallicana*) which was revised and approved by a synod at Paris, delivered by Theodore Beza to Charles IX at Poissy in 1561, and later adopted by the Synod of La Rochelle in 1571.

In that same year on Christmas day Calvin was officially granted by the Little Council the title of "bourgeois of Geneva"—in a real sense already *his* city for whose spiritual benefit he had been laboring and praying for almost twenty-five years.

Calvin's French translation of his 1559 Latin edition of the *Institutes* was published in 1560. He himself translated only the first seven chapters of Book One. An unknown translator or translators did the rest. Also, in 1560 Philip Melanchthon, the Lutheran "Preceptor of Germany," died.

Four fruitful years later, throughout which he continued to preach from the pulpit of St. Peter's Church and to write his commentaries on Daniel (1561) and Jeremiah and Lamentations (1563), Calvin followed his Lutheran friend to glory. Though generally healthy in his youth and young manhood, Calvin in his thirties, due to his study habits, had begun increasingly to experience physical ailments of one kind or another, becoming a chronic sufferer from ague, catarrh (inflammation of the mucous membrane in the nose which caused continual nose-running), asthma, indigestion, and migraine headache. In 1558 he had a long illness of quartan fever (an intermittent malarial fever) from which he never fully recovered. Suffering also from arthritis, ulcerous hemorrhoids, gum disease, and pleurisy that led finally to malignant tuberculosis, his body was constantly wracked with pain. So his death was his deliverance into that state that the apostle Paul described as only "gain" and "better by far" than this one (Phil. 1:21, 23).

He preached his last sermon from the pulpit of St. Peter's Church on February 6, 1564 and attended church for the last time there on Easter Sunday, April 20. On April 27, at his request, the Little Council came to his home where he thanked them for their many kindnesses to him, asked their pardon for his occasional outbursts of temper toward them, and exhorted them to remain faithful to pure doctrine.

On May 2 he wrote and informed Farel of his physical condition, this being the last letter he ever penned:

> Farewell, my best and truest friend! And since it is God's will that you remain behind me in this world, live mindful of our friendship, which as it was useful to the Church of God, so the fruit of it awaits us in heaven. Pray do not fatigue yourself on my account. It is with difficulty that I draw my breath, and I expect that every moment will be the last. It is enough that I live and die for Christ, who is the reward of his followers both in life and in death. Again, farewell with the brethren.[18]

In spite of Calvin's wish that Farel not "fatigue himself" by visiting him, the aged Reformer made his way to Geneva for a touching farewell visit with his old friend. He did not stay for Calvin's death but returned home.

During the last week of his life Calvin called the Venerable Company of Pastors to his bedside and told the sorrowing pastors among other things:

> I have had many faults that you had to tolerate, and all that I accomplished was of little significance. The evil-minded will take advantage of this confession, but I repeat that all that I have done is of little significance, and I am a poor creature. My faults have always displeased me and the root of the fear of the Lord has always been in my heart. As for my doctrine, I have taught faithfully, and God has given me grace to write, which I have done faithfully as I could; and I have not corrupted [or mutilated] one single passage of Scripture nor twisted it as far as I know; and when in a position to arrive at an artificial meaning through subtlety, I have put all that under my feet, and have always aimed at being simple. *I have written nothing out of hatred against anyone*, but have always set before me what I thought was for the glory of God.[19]

On April 25 he dictated his will and on May 27 died of pulmonary tuberculosis, six weeks before his fifty-fifth birthday, the year after Rome's Council of Trent ended, having lived fifty-four years, ten months, and seventeen days.

He was buried the next day. Theodore Beza officiated at his funeral. At his request, Calvin was buried in an unmarked grave. Today, no one knows for certain where this great Reformation leader—the author of seventy-one volumes of some of the finest theological writing in existence and the most hated, reviled, and feared of all of Rome's enemies in his own time—is buried. Today tour guides will point out to tourists a grave stone marked "J C" but whether it actually

---

[18]Calvin, *Works*, XX, 302.

[19]*Corpus Reformatorum*, 9, 893b (emphasis supplied).

marks Calvin's burial site is uncertain. His life's testimony
may be summed up in what Philip Schaff argues is Calvin's
own poetic composition, written in French and discovered
by Felix Bovet of Neuchâtel in an old Genevan prayer book
of 1545, which appeared in the Geneva Psalter of 1551.[20]
We sing that poem today in our churches in English
translation using these words:

> I greet thee, who my sure Redeemer art,
> My only trust and Saviour of my heart,
> Who pain didst undergo for my poor sake;
> I pray thee from our hearts all cares to take.
>
> Thou art the King of mercy and of grace,
> Reigning omnipotent in ev'ry place;
> So come, O King, and our whole being sway;
> Shine on us with the light of thy pure day.
>
> Thou art the Life, by which alone we live,
> And all our substance and our strength receive;
> O comfort us in death's approaching hour,
> Strong hearted then to face it by thy pow'r.
>
> Thou hast the true and perfect gentleness,
> No harshness hast thou and no bitterness:
> Make us to taste the sweet grace found in thee
> And ever stay in thy sweet unity.
>
> Our hope is in no other save in thee;
> Our faith is built upon thy promise free;
> O grant to us such stronger hope and sure
> That we can boldly conquer and endure.

---

[20]Philip Schaff, *History of the Christian Church* (Third revised
edition; Grand Rapids: Eerdmans, 1910), VIII, 842-43.

If this is in fact Calvin's composition (admittedly, some authorities dispute that it is)[21] it is a fitting tribute in verse to the living faith and theological thought of John Calvin.

CONCLUDING APPLICATION

Émile Doumergue, the renowned French biographer of Calvin, did not permit the evident fact of God's marvelous providence in the preparation of Calvin for his life's task to pass without some comment:

> Driven from Noyon by the plague while still little more than a child, he falls in with the best teacher of Latin of the age, Mathurin Cordier, who waits before leaving Paris to teach him. Then at Orléans he falls in with the best master of Greek of the age, Melchior Wolmar, who seems to have come from Germany, whither he is about to return, in order to inculcate his method upon him.

---

[21] As further testimony to the ascription of this hymn to Calvin, *Opera*, volume 6, of the 1868 edition of Calvin's works includes the French text of this hymn. Nevertheless, scholars deny that Calvin wrote it primarily because they allege that the text appears to be a Protestant version of the Roman Catholic hymn, "Salve Regina," and because Calvin (unlike Luther) left no heritage of adapting Roman Catholic texts to his liturgy for his own purpose. It is, however, a real stretch for anyone to argue that the text of this Geneva hymn is an adaptation of "Salve Regina" whose text reads:

Hail holy queen, mother of mercy,
    Hail our life, our sweetness and our hope.
To you do we cry, poor banished children of Eve,
    To you do we send up our sighs, mourning and weeping
        in this valley of tears.
Turn then, most gracious advocate,
    your eyes of mercy toward us.
And after this, our exile,
    Show us the fruit of your womb, Jesus,
    O clement, O loving, O sweet Virgin Mary.

Two incomparable masters who prove incomparable instructors. Not content with teaching him the languages they speak to him the Gospel of Christ.

It was for him, it seems, that the Middle Ages had preserved the somber college of Montaigu, so that before it disappeared it might initiate him into all the secrets of an irresistible dialectic [Doumergue has reference here to the Nominalist philosophy of Duns Scotus, William of Occam, Gabriel Biel, and, above all, to the *Sentences* of Peter Lombard]. For him too it was that modern times had hastened to establish the College of France, that he might attend its first lectures and later rank among the masters of humanism.

And even this is not enough: here is our young man encountering the most illustrious professors of law,—l'Estoile, who is still at Orléans, and Alciat, who has just arrived at Bourges. They mold his mind to that kind of precise, exact, realistic thinking which permits him to be not merely the theologian but the legislator of the Reformation.

Nevertheless Providence had not yet accomplished more than half its task. What is intellect without life? And these wonderful years of study are at the same time wonderful years of experience. The church takes care to reveal to him all its failings, all its most secret vices. It gives him personal experience of its weaknesses and its hardnesses. It endows him abusively with its benefices; it casts him unjustly into prison [in Noyon]; it obliges him to rescue the dead body of his father from its anathemas. While yet a babe he commences to visit the bizarre relics of Ourscamp; later he looks upon the episcopal disorders at Angoulême; he listens to the legends of Poitiers [about the footprints of Christ in the chapel of the Church of St. Radegonde who purportedly appeared to the saint in 587, and two fragments of Peter's jawbone and a portion of his beard in the Cathedral itself].

But by the side of the shadow destined to repel him shines the light destined to attract him. If Calvin was the pupil of Béda, chief of the Sorbonnic band, he is also the *protégé* of the friends of Le Fèvre d'Etaple, the Cops and the Budés.... He allies himself intimately with Gérard Roussel, and the venerable Le Fèvre prolongs his life to more than a century that he may be able to give him his blessing at Nérac. Similarly before enduring his martyrdom, Estienne de la Forge receives him into his house and permits him to learn the piety and heroism of the nascent Church, while Quintin, chief of Libertines, and Servetus, chief of Antitrinitarians, present themselves in Paris to horrify the young doctor with their dangerous heresies.[22]

As I bring this lecture series on the life of John Calvin now to a close, I would urge you to see with eyes of faith that same marvelous providential leading and working that was at work in Calvin's life at work in your life as well. Your reading these chapters God arranged for some reason. If you do not see it now, it will all come clear some day, in or after *your* battles!

I would also urge you to take your church's history more seriously than you have in the past and to begin to research and to learn it. And, oh yes, get your personal copy of Calvin's *Institutes* (and Battles' helpful *Analysis of the Institutes*), carefully read it, mark it, and digest its great theology. Then, if you reject his theology after you have done so, be prepared, as Battles enjoins, to offer a comparable alternative in its stead to the world.

Finally, I would urge you to thank God for the theological giants that walked the earth during the sixteenth century— Luther, Melanchthon, Bucer, Zwingli, Bullinger, Farel, Calvin, Beza, Knox—on whose shoulders we stand today. Perhaps such a one is again being prepared right now at a theological seminary somewhere who could use your friendship, your prayers, and your tangible enablements. Investigate and become involved in the training of these future Reformers for the spiritual benefit of your children's generation and for the conversion of a needy, lost and dying world.

---

[22]Doumergue, *Jean Calvin. Les hommes et les choses de son temps*, 1, 14-15.

OPPOSING CALVIN BIOGRAPHERS

John Calvin has naturally had his biographical detractors
from Roman Catholic scholars through the centuries on the
one hand to theologically liberal and neo-orthodox scholars
in more recent times on the other. The following are the
more significant detractors in these two categories, all
drawn from Richard Stauffer's *The Humanness of John
Calvin*, translated by George Shriver with a foreword by
John T. McNeill [Nashville, TN: Abingdon, 1971, 20-30]:

ROMAN CATHOLIC BIOGRAPHERS

(a) Jérome-Hermès Bolsec, a Carmelite physician who
converted to Protestantism, fell out with Calvin over his view
of predestination and returned to the Roman church.

In his *L'Historie de la vie, moeurs, actes, doctrine,
constance et mort de Jean Calvin, jadis ministre de Genève*
(1577; an edition was published in Paris in 1835), he accuses
Calvin of being ambitious, presumptuous, arrogant, cruel,
evil, vindictive, avaricious, greedy, and ignorant; an imposter
and charlatan who claimed he could raise the dead; a lover
of rich fare and a bi-sexual who indulged sexually with any
and every female within walking distance and for whose
homosexual habits his birth city of Noyon had sentenced
him to be branded with a hot iron; and who, as an outcast of
God, was "eaten with lice and vermin all over his body,"
wasted away as punishment for his sins, and died cursing
and swearing as a blasphemer.

(b) Florimond de Raemond, counselor of the Parlement of
Bordeaux, in his *Historie de la naissance, progrez ed*

decadence de l'hérésie de ce siècle (Paris, 1605) calls Calvin's *Institutes* "the Koran or rather the Talmud of Heresy, being, as it is, a mass of all errors that have ever existed in the past, or ever will exist, I verily believe, in the future."

(c) Jacques Desmay, vicar-general of the diocese of Rouen, in his *Remarques sur la vie de Jean Calvin, tirees des registres de Noyon, ville de sa naissance* (Rouen, 1621) characterizes Calvin as "the author of a religion of the table, the stomach, the fat, the flesh, the kitchen," in whom the whole Reformation tended to "establish the reign of wine, women, and song." He also says Calvin was a thief.

(d) Bossuet, Bishop of Meaux, in his *Histoire des variations des Eglises protestantes* (1688; an edition was published in Paris in 1828) accuses Calvin of being very ambitious, autocratic, a man with a quick temper and a morose and bitter spirit, showing "serious sickness" in the way he pursued his adversaries with sarcasm.

(e) J. M. Audin in his *Histoire de la vie, des ouvrages et des doctrines de Calvin* (Paris, 1841, 1856) accuses Calvin of cowardice, an unfeeling heart, deceit, egocentrism, and despotism: "Calvin never loved,[1] and no one loved him either. One dreaded him, one feared him. No one felt drawn to him because of personal appeal. All those who knew him withdrew from him because they could not tolerate his arrogant way, his sick egoism, his vain outbursts, his unmeasured pride." Audin declares that Calvin was stricken with and died of a shameful disease.

---

[1]This is a ludicrous statement. Evidence abounds that Calvin loved and was loved in return by his intimate associates. His concern for others is also apparent, to cite just one example, in the famous letter he wrote to the five condemned missionary prisoners at Lyons on June 10, 1552.

(f) F. W. Kampshulte, professor at the University of Bonn, in his *Johann Calvin: seine Kirche und sein Staat in Genf* (Leipzig, 1899) is much more moderating and sober in his depiction of Calvin, but he still speaks of him as the "discreet and grave ecclesiastic from gloomy Chanoines [Canons] Street."

(g) André Favre-Dorsaz in his *Calvin et Loyola: deux Réformes* (Paris and Brussels, 1951) represents Calvin as acidic, negative, withdrawn, embittered, unfeeling, and pessimistic; as an uneasy, worried, anguished, and cruel man who was proud, sadistic, and dictatorial; as a superficial theologian [!], a tendentious exegete, and a believer in whom "religious feeling" was of a rather doubtful quality,[2] who believed more in law than he did in grace, who did not know how to pray,[3] and who did not understand the spirit of Jesus.

---

[2]To say that it is doubtful that Calvin had any "religious feeling" totally ignores the material of *Institutes*, 3.6-10, "The Life of the Christian Man." John T. McNeill in *Calvin: Institutes of the Christian Religion*, edited by John T. McNeill (Philadelphia: Westminster, 1960), 1, lx, says of this section, published separately as early as 1550 as *The Golden Booklet of the Christian Life* and the first portion of the *Institutes* to be translated into English, that it is "balanced, penetrating, and practical." This criticism also ignores the pastor's heart often revealed in Calvin's letters.

[3]Like virtually all of the other criticisms that are being listed in this appendix, this statement is simply absurd. To say that Calvin did not know how to pray completely ignores *Institutes*, 3.20, a chapter about which McNeill in *Calvin: Institutes of the Christian Religion*, 2, 850, fn 1, writes:

This thoughtful and ample chapter, with its tone of devout warmth, takes its place in the forefront of historically celebrated discussions of prayer, such as Tertullian's *De oratione*..., Origen, Nχπý χσταφη ..., Gregory of Nyssa, *On the Lord's Prayer*..., and the short treatises of Augustine...and of Hugh of St. Victor.

He declares: "Calvin promised much more than he could produce. He did not possess, as strongly as he thought, the 'key to open' the Holy Scripture…. Doubtless it is less a question of reflecting on the authentic meaning of Scripture than of insisting long and hard and of gaining power of the reform party. The *Institutes* is the theology of a hurried layman, of an amateur lawyer, who has finally found the aim of his self-satisfaction."

He goes on, of course, to eulogize Loyola, the founder of the Society of Jesus (the Jesuit Order), whose order makes virtues of its doctrines of blind allegiance to the papacy, "intentionalism" (its doctrine that the end justifies the means), "mental reservation" (its doctrine that a man is not obliged to state the whole truth under oath), and "probablism" (its doctrine that the probability of a thing makes it a good thing).

(h) Daniel-Rops in his *Histoire de l'Eglise du Christ* (Paris, 1955) describes Calvin as a genius, containing "something terrible and cold," with an exterior that was "cold and powerful," from which emanated a kind of Faustian charm which made him "the perfect type of fanatic," a dictator who loved few, if any, men "in their wretchedness and weakness."

LIBERAL AND NEO-ORTHODOX BIOGRAPHERS

(a) Jacques Aug. and his son Jean-Barthelemy Galiffe in their respective volumes, *Matériaux pour l'historie de Genève*, 2 vols. (1829, 1830), and *Besançon Hugues, libérateur de Genève. Historique de la fondation de l'independence Genevoise* (1859), reflecting the bitterness that several old Genevese families felt toward Calvin, depict him as a foreigner, an intruder, and usurper of the life of the city.

(b) Alfred Franklin, a liberal nineteenth-century theologian, in his "Introduction" to *La Vie de J. Calvin* by Theodore Beza (Paris, 1869) pictures Calvin as "this great black phantom, a glacial person, sombre, unfeeling, prey to an exclusive idea, who moved through the world quickly and left upon it a deep mark, [who] irresistibly drew attention without inspiring sympathy. One resists his ascendancy, because he cannot satisfy reason and nothing in him speaks to the heart." He says still further about the Reformer that he was a man of "austerity without enthusiasm, an unfeeling and cold heart, never showing emotion. Did he ever laugh, did he ever cry?" Still further Franklin writes that Calvin was a despot who stopped the "magnificent outburst which the word of Luther had started throughout Europe," who never understood the "very essence of Christianity." Finally, he says of Calvin that, except for his *Institutes*, his books are "unreadable": "He is not a thinker. He lacks the quality of eagerly seeking truth and the ideal of never ceasing to search and doubt"; "His thought, incapable of embracing an ensemble of abstract ideas, of tracing out important lines and then determining general laws, excels in dialectics, an exercise full of details and demanding agility rather than an understanding mind"; a man of "strong personality rather than a strong understanding."

(c) Oskar Pfïster, a neo-orthodox pastor and Freudian psychologist in Zürich, in his *Calvins Eingreifen in die Hexer- and Hexenprozesse von Peny 1545 nach seiner Bedeutung für Geschichte und Gegenwart* (Zürich, 1947), clinically psychoanalyzes Calvin 383 years after his death in Freudian categories and concludes that he was a pitiable victim of compulsive neuroses, a sadist without love in whom cruelty and hate were born from a morbid anguish. Incidentally, Hartmann Grisar did a similar psychoanalysis of Martin Luther with similar results.

(d) Stefan Zweig, an Austrian novelist, wrote *Castellio gegen Calvin, oder ein Gewissen gegen die Gewalt* (Vienna, 1936), a book that was judged by Roland de Pury as "one of the most downright pernicious falsehoods ever produced in historical literature."

(e) Jean Schroder, a former pastor of St. Peters Cathedral in Geneva, who had urged Zweig to write his book, felt it necessary to write *Jean Calvin et sa dictature d'après des historiens anciens et modernes* (Geneva, 1948) in which he portrays Calvin simply as a dictator, based upon such facts as men of Geneva referring to him as "master" rather than as "brother." Of course, men of learning were commonly so addressed.

Admittedly, Calvin was not perfect by any means; indeed, he had a fierce temper, doubtless often provoked by his migraine headaches. But evidence indicates that he regularly sought advice from the members of the Little Council and his fellow ministers in Geneva and was neither a dictator nor did he desire to be one.

Sober Calvin scholars have responded to these negative depictions of Calvin through the years and answered them. But in light of such calumnies, how does one go about discovering the truth about Calvin for oneself? I would suggest a trip through his letters. There one will see Calvin is all his humanness as a husband and father, as a friend and pastor. One source in particular that is quite helpful in this regard is Henry F. Henderson's *Calvin in His Letters* (Reprint; Eugene, OR: Wipf & Stock, 1996), that shows that the more one becomes acquainted with the real Calvin through his letters the stronger becomes one's respect for him, not only because of his great intellectual gifts and accomplishments but also because of his equally great humanness.

A MAJOR INFLUENCE OF CALVINISM ON WESTERN HISTORY

The successful insistence of Calvin on the separation of the church from the state and the state from the church (the "free church in a free state" principle) in order that Jesus might exercise his kingly rights in his church has had, I would suggest, another major influence—little recognized today but one that current events would suggest we ought to take quite seriously—on the last five hundred years of Western history. And that influence is this: during the medieval age the world of Islam had moved to the forefront of human civilization and achievement while Western Europe had become a small and unimportant appendage of the vast continent of Eurasia. John W. Robbins writes:

> As the greatest political, military, economic, and religious power on Earth, Islam's global triumph seemed inevitable. The battles in Europe that the Europeans thought so decisive, such as [Charles Martel's victory at] Tours in northern France in 732, only a century after Muhammad's death, were regarded as minor setbacks by the Muslims. Rather, they saw their inexorable advance reflected in the ignominious expulsion of the Catholic Crusaders from the Levant in the 13th century, the capture of Constantinople in 1453, and their triumphant march through the Balkans toward Vienna in the early 17th century.[1]

But for some reason Islam did not absorb these "backward peoples" of the West. What happened to stop Islam's

---

[1]John W. Robbins in his *Book Review* of Bernard Lewis, *What Went Wrong?* (Oxford University Press, 2002) in *The Trinity Review* 213 (November 2002), 4.

conquest of all of Eurasia? Islam's failure to conquer Europe was not due to its military weakness or to the military strength of the Europeans. In fact, as Robbins notes:

> Many in [western] Christendom welcomed the Muslims (which partly explains Islam's rapid expanse) as offering more freedom than the Roman ecclesiocracy of Western Europe permitted. The Orthodox Patriarch of Constantinople said, "Rather the turban of the Turk than the tiara of the Pope," and refugees from the tyranny of papal Rome flowed for centuries into Muslim lands.[2]

Indeed, to cite Bernard Lewis, Dodge Professor of Near Eastern Studies at Princeton University, directly:

> The medieval Islamic world offered only limited freedom in comparison with modern ideals and even with modern practice in the more advanced democracies, but it offered vastly more freedom than any of its predecessors, its contemporaries and most of its successors.[3]

That correlation of Islam's even limited freedom with civilization is the key to understanding the reason Islam was the acme of human civilization a thousand years ago. But it is not that today. Five hundred years ago something changed. What was that? Not Islam, but the West itself! Lewis observes:

> A principle cause of Western progress [in the sixteenth century was] the separation of church and state....the idea that [institutionalized] religion and political authority, church and state are different, and can or should be separated—is in a profound sense, Christian.[4]

Unfortunately, Lewis does not develop this idea but he provides many illustrations of how the resurgence of Protestant

[2]Robbins, *Review* of Lewis, *What Went Wrong?* in *The Trinity Review*, 4.
[3]Bernard Lewis, *What Went Wrong?*, 156.
[4]Lewis, *What Went Wrong?*, 96.

Christianity (I would say, particularly in its Calvinistic form) in the sixteenth century and the growth of learning that prepared the way for, accompanied, and was the result of the Reformation transformed the West and gave it new power and reasons to resist the spread of Islam, not by the sword but by the spread and appeal of the biblical gospel.

In sum, Islam's triumphant global march was halted by the sudden appearance of the freedom fostered by biblical Christianity in the sixteenth century in Western Europe. This occurred particularly as a result of Calvin's, not Luther's, insistence on the church's freedom from the state and the state's freedom from the church that in turn also eventually produced disciplined capitalism, science and technology, and economic prosperity. In yet another way, then—in the political freedom the Western nations enjoy now over against what would have possibly been military subjection to an Islamic theocracy—we here in the West are indebted to the providentially-arranged thought and activity of John Calvin.

APPENDIX C

RECOMMENDED CALVIN BIOGRAPHIES

The literature on John Calvin is immense. Thousands of books, essays, and journal articles primarily in French, German, and English have been written about the man. The best Calvin libraries are in the University of Geneva where his manuscripts are preserved in excellent order and in the St. Thomasstift at Strasbourg.[1] One may consult John T. McNeill's bibliographical essay, "Fifty Years of Calvin Study" (1918-1968) in Williston Walker's *John Calvin: The Organiser of Reformed Protestantism* (New York: Schocken, 1969), xvii-lxxvii, to get some idea just how immense the Calvin literature still is. Walker himself in his "Bibliographical Note," ix-xvi, also provides some guidance here. Both single out the significance of Émile Doumergue's seven-volume biography of Calvin that was published over the period of time spanning 1899 to 1927 although both note that one must be aware that Calvin is clearly Doumergue's hero and that he is therefore "led into occasional exaggeration by his enthusiasm" (Walker) for his subject.

For beginning English readers who are interested in reading more about John Calvin I would recommend the following biographies and articles:

Theodore Beza, *The Life of John Calvin* (Edinburgh: Calvin Translation Society, 1844). Beza is the earliest Calvin biographer, writing in fact two biographies of Calvin, the first originally in French in 1564, the second originally in

---

[1] In America the Meeter Collection at Calvin College, Grand Rapids, Michigan, alone has around 14,000 articles on Calvin.

Latin in 1575. A purported third biography by Beza in 1565 was actually written by Nicolas Colladon.

Bernard Cottret, *Calvin: A Biography*, translated by M. Wallace McDonald (Grand Rapids: Eerdmans, 2000). Beginning students of Calvin may want to postpone reading Cottret's biography until they have digested two or three other biographies on my list. But sooner or later they must read Cottret's work. It is a *tour de force*. He provides a select Calvin bibliography, 356-64.

W. Gary Crampton, *What Calvin Says: An Introduction to the Theology of John Calvin* (Jefferson, Maryland: Trinity Foundation, 1992). While this book is, strictly speaking, not a biography as such, it does provide some biographical information about Calvin and introduces the theological novice to the theological thought of Calvin.

Jacob T. Hoogstra (ed.), *John Calvin: Contemporary Prophet* (Philadelphia: Presbyterian and Reformed, 1959). This is a symposium of articles by fifteen contributors, including Pierre Marcel, William Childs Robinson, W. Stanford Reid, John H. Gerstner, Philip Edgcumbe Hughes, Gerrit C. Berkouwer, and C. Gregg Singer.

Robert Nigel Carew Hunt, *Calvin* (London: Centenary, 1933). As a biography it is unsurpassed, but Hunt is somewhat hard at times on Calvin because of his doctrine of predestination.

Alister E. McGrath, *A Life of John Calvin* (Grand Rapids: Baker, 1990). McGrath's biography is very good, providing some original details about Calvin's education.

John T. McNeill, *The History and Character of Calvinism* (New York: Oxford, 1954), 93-234. This work is both a biography of Calvin and a very good description of the history and character of Calvinism as a theological system.

James I. Packer, "Calvin the Theologian," in *John Calvin: A Collection of Distinguished Essays*, edited by G. D. Duffield (Grand Rapids: Eerdmans, 1966).

T. H. L. Parker, *Portrait of Calvin* (London: SCM, 1940). This biography is short and quite readable. It would be my first recommendation for beginning students.

T. H. L. Parker, *John Calvin* (Batavoa, Illinois: King, 1975). In my opinion, this biography of Calvin is one of the best. Parker is not afraid to suggest original interpretations of Calvin.

C. Gregg Singer, *John Calvin: His Roots and Fruits* (Philadelphia: Presbyterian and Reformed, 1967). Short but informative.

Emanuel Stickelberger, *John Calvin*, translated by David Georg Gelzer (Reprint; Cambridge: James Clarke, 1977). Stickelberger's biography is very readable, offers a lively portrait of Calvin, and is obviously intent on "rescuing Calvin from his antagonistic biographers" (McNeill).

Williston Walker, *John Calvin: The Organiser of Reformed Protestantism* (New York: Schocken, 1906). This biography is truly a classic and quite scholarly. The beginner must not be put off by my comment concerning its evident scholarship for it is elegantly written and makes for easy reading.

Benjamin B. Warfield, "John Calvin: The Man and His Work," in *The Works of Benjamin B. Warfield* (Reprint; Grand Rapids: Baker, 1991), V, 3-26; "John Calvin the Theologian" and "The Theology of Calvin," both in *Calvin and Augustine*, edited by Samuel G. Craig (Philadelphia: Presbyterian and Reformed, 1956), 481-7 and 487-95 respectively; "What is Calvinism?," "Calvin and the Bible," and "Calvin and the Reformation," all three in *Selected Shorter Writings of*

Benjamin B. Warfield, edited by John E. Meeter (Nutley, New Jersey: Presbyterian and Reformed, 1970), I, 389-92, 397-400, 401-6 respectively.

There are other Calvin biographies in English, of course, but these I have listed will serve well anyone who desires to read more about Calvin beyond these lectures. These biographies in turn will list other authors and titles that may be consulted as one's interest in Calvin expands.

General Index

Other books of Interest
from
Christian Focus

ROBERT L. REYMOND

The

REFORMATION'S
CONFLICT
WITH ROME
Why it Must Continue

FOREWORD BY R.C. SPROUL

THE REFORMATION'S CONFLICT WITH ROME
Why it Must Continue
Robert L Reymond
Foreword by R.C. Sproul

'*Dr. Reymond clearly demonstrates in this monograph that there are several serious doctrinal differences between Roman Catholic teaching and Biblical Christianity... I am confident the reader will find this work clear, fair and accurate. I highly commend its close reading.*'

Dr. R.C. Sproul,
Ligonier Ministries, Orlando, Florida

'*The Christian public is indebted to Dr. Reymond for producing such a lucid and incisive volume evaluating modern attempts to rejoin Protestant churches with the Roman Catholic Church... The reader will be well-informed by this decisive, but irenic, rejection of the notion that the Roman church has always embraced the biblical concept of justification by faith.*'

Dr. Richard L. Mayhue,
The Master's Seminary, Sun Valley, California

'*Robert Reymond is to be warmly commended for producing such a lucid book on the Reformation controversy with Rome, and why that controversy must continue even today.*'

Dr. Nick Needham,
Highland Theological College, Dingwall, Scotland

Written in an inoffensive yet honest way, Robert Reymond has studied the essential divisions between Roman Catholics and the Reformed church to find out the real issues and points of conflict.

Reymond looks at historical watersheds of doctrine, the development of Roman Catholic authority and contemporary attempts at rapprochement (including *'Evangelicals and Catholics Together'* and Robert Sungenis' *'Not by Faith Alone'*). In doing so he helps us understand the great truths of salvation worked out through the sacrifice of Jesus, the Messiah.

ISBN 978-1-85792-626-2

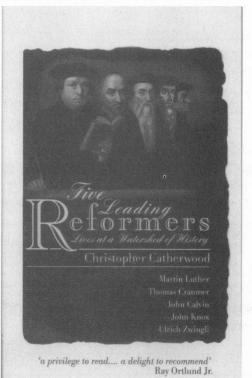

Five
Leading
Reformers
Lives at a Watershed of History

Christopher Catherwood

Martin Luther
Thomas Cranmer
John Calvin
John Knox
Ulrich Zwingli

'a privilege to read.... a delight to recommend'
Ray Ortlund Jr.

FIVE LEADING REFORMERS

Lives at a Watershed of History

Christopher Catherwood

'*Christopher Catherwood, a writer abreast of ongoing historical study of the period and aware of the spiritual issues hanging
on the chain of events, track five major players from the cradle
to the grave: Luther, Zwingli, Calvin, Cranmer, Knox. Each in his
way was a watershed figure, and Catherwood's vivid profiling of
them will help to keep their memory green.*'

**Dr. J.I. Packer
Regent College, Vancouver**

'*He shows how five men of very different personality and out-
look could all be caught up in the same experience of a life transformed by the power of God.*'

**Dr. Gerald Bray
Beeson Divinity School, Samford Univerity,
Birmingham, Alabama**

'*.. shows how their lives were touched by greatness from God,
for He must be the ultimate explanation for the reformers' accomplishments. As I read, I was constantly making connections
with our present-day situation.*'

**Dr. Ray Ortlund Jr.,
First Presbyterian Church, Augusta, Georgia**

'*The author emphasises especially the political dimension of the
reformation, and with it the emancipation of lay people. This is a
religious biography with a message for today, lest we forget.*'

**The late Dr. David Wright,
New College, Edinburgh**

Christopher Catherwood is an Historian and author from Cambridge,
England

ISBN 978-1-85792-507-4

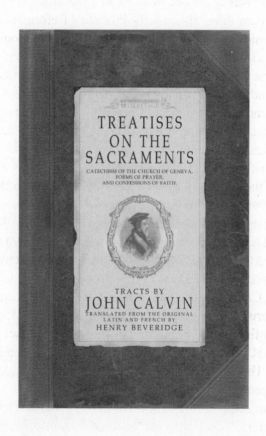

TREATISES
ON THE
SACRAMENTS

CATECHISM OF THE CHURCH OF GENEVA,
FORMS OF PRAYER,
AND CONFESSIONS OF FAITH.

TRACTS BY
JOHN CALVIN
TRANSLATED FROM THE ORIGINAL
LATIN AND FRENCH BY
HENRY BEVERIDGE

Treatises on the Sacraments

Calvin's Tracts translated by Henry Beveridge

John Calvin

John Calvin was easily one of the most influential Christians of the 2nd millennium. A key figure in the Protestant Reformation, Calvin's legacy remains immensely strong, with hundreds of thousands gaining insights from his works of major doctrines such as the interaction between the Sovereignty of God and Man's Free Will. Countless analyses and critiques of Calvin's work have been released over the centuries, and a huge number of Churches and denominations hold to Calvin's teaching to varying degrees. Calvin's name is thrown about in theological discussions covering a broad spectrum, we may know the Calvinist's view, but what does Calvin himself say?

One of the key issues that led to the reformation and the birth of Protestantism was Rome's treatment of the Lord's Supper. This is the main subject of this collection of Calvin's tracts. Calvin and the Reformers believed the Catholic Mass was founded on a grave error that needed to be corrected. According to Rome's doctrine of transubstantiation the bread and wine supernaturally became Christ's body and blood. Calvin on the other hand held that they were symbolic and to say otherwise bordered on idolatry and diminished Christ's once for all sacrifice on the cross. This key point of difference remains to this day and Calvin's writings have become a starting point from which Reformed Theologians have gone on to defend and develop the Protestant stance.

This unedited collection of sermons allows you to read John Calvin's own ideas on issues relating to the sacraments, catechisms, forms of prayer and confessions of faith.

'*...there is no substitute for going to the sources themselves. For English readers interested in the sacramental theology of John Calvin, this volume provides a most beneficial resource.*'

Dr. Keith A. Mathison,
Ligonier Ministries, Orlando, Florida

ISBN 978-1-85792-725-2

Christian Focus Publications

publishes books for all ages

Our mission statement –

STAYING FAITHFUL
In dependence upon God we seek to help make His infallible Word,
the Bible, relevant. Our aim is to ensure that the Lord Jesus Christ is
presented as the only hope to obtain forgiveness of sin, live a useful
life and look forward to heaven with Him.

REACHING OUT
Christ's last command requires us to reach out to our world with His
gospel. We seek to help fulfill that by publishing books that point people
towards Jesus and help them develop a Christ-like maturity. We aim
to equip all levels of readers for life, work, ministry and mission.

Books in our adult range are published in three imprints.
Christian Focus contains popular works including biographies,
commentaries, basic doctrine and Christian living. Our children's
books are also published in this imprint.
Mentor focuses on books written at a level suitable for Bible
College and seminary students, pastors, and other serious readers. The imprint includes commentaries, doctrinal studies, ex-
amination of current issues and church history.
Christian Heritage contains classic writings from the past.

For a free catalogue of all our titles, please write to
Christian Focus Publications, Ltd
Geanies House, Fearn,
Ross-shire, IV20 1TW, Scotland, United Kingdom
info@christianfocus.com

For details of our titles visit us on our website
www.christianfocus.com